The Green Card Guidebook

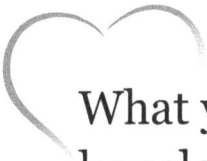

What you *must know* if you're falling hopelessly in love with a foreigner!

**By Clare Corado,
Immigration Attorney**

Trompeta Press

Library of Congress Control Number: 2015919449

ISBN 978-0-9970638-0-6 (pbk) – ISBN 978-0-9970638-1-3 (ebook)

Please note:

The information in this book is not legal advice and is not intended to enable the reader solve legal problems or represent themselves or others in immigration matters. Consult a knowledgeable attorney licensed to practice in your jurisdiction for personalized advice.

Acknowledgements

Many thanks to my husband and children for their patience and support as I wrote this book.

I am also especially grateful to the wonderful mentors who taught me how to practice law, as well as to the immigration lawyer who obtained a green card for my husband so many years ago. Our life together was made possible by your work!

About the Author

Clare Corado became an immigration attorney after going through a nightmare-ish green card case with her husband Marcial. She is the founder of Corado Immigration Law, a law firm dedicated to helping Americans get U.S. citizenship for their foreign spouses.

Clare is a nationally-recognized lecturer on immigration law for other attorneys. She has lobbied Congress for immigration reform and had her work published in Legal Ink Magazine. Her clients appreciate the fact that she speaks fluent Spanish.

Clare loves to hear from her readers and welcomes suggestions for future editions of this book.

You can contact her at **www.CoradoLaw.com**.

Table of Contents

Love: the Foundation of Your Case 9

What?! No Automatic Green Card?... 13

- The #1 immigration urban legend of all time
- A snapshot of the journey ahead
- Eeny-meeny-miny-moh: choosing which path to take

How Thinking Ahead Makes It 300% Easier............................ 23

- 5 Things to Start Saving Right Now
- Key actions USCIS thinks "real" couples take
- Do I really have to change my last name?

Timing is Everything 29

- Crystal balls and other ways to guess how long it will take
- My "Happy Healthy" Worksheet
- Tips for planning a timeline-neutral wedding

The Marriage Interview 35

- Debunking top internet rumors
- The no-longer-secret USCIS list of red flags
- An insider's compilation of the classic questions

What's Next? 43

- Every journey starts with the first step
- How to choose your lawyer

Final Thoughts 47

BONUS: Transcripts of Clare's popular "Immigration for Couples" 5-part seminar series

Part 1: Marriage Immigration Options 101

Part 2: Potential Pitfalls, aka "Grounds of Inadmissibility"

Part 3: Overcoming the Obstacles with Waivers

Part 4: How to Plan Around Tricky Immigration Timelines

Part 5: The Marriage Interview: Truth vs Urban Legend

Love: the foundation of your case

Section 1

Love: the foundation of your case

Congratulations on finding the person you want to spend the rest of your life with! I am so happy for you, and I wish you a long life together.

Every couple has a unique journey, with unique joys and challenges.

Because you are reading this book, I'm betting one of the unique parts of your relationship is your multiculturalism.

Each of you brings different experiences, life views, and maybe even different languages to the relationship. And your mash-up of cooking styles probably makes for some amazing dinner parties!

However, as a multi-national couple you will face some unique challenges as well. If you've decided to make your home together in the United States, one of these challenges will be going through the U.S. immigration process.

But before we talk details, there is one very important thing I want you to keep in mind:

This journey is not easy, but it's absolutely worth it!

Think of the immigration process as the foundation you two will build your lives together on.

From the very beginning, it is so important that you both have a clear image in your minds of the life that you are working towards.

Holding that image in your mind helps you remember why you are doing all of this in the first place. It will help you keep perspective during all of the little frustrations that may come up during your case.

Think for a minute about the plans you have for your future life together:

- Where will you live?
- What will you be doing?
- What is your lifestyle like?
- What will your relationship be like over the years?

- Do you want to have kids, or maybe a dog that you treat like your kid?

- What will you do to contribute to society?

I bet the two of you have talked this through in a lot of detail before, but I want you to bring the image of your future life to the forefront of your mind, in vibrant color and high definition.

So put a piece of paper or your phone at this spot in the book to hold your place, and close your eyes for a moment so you can picture more clearly your future life.

I'd also encourage you to take the time to work this out on paper in more detail later to clarify your vision further. Talk with your fiancé/husband/wife and have fun creating vision this together.

❤ ❤ ❤

Why are we talking about this in a book about getting a green card?

Because it is CRUCIAL that you keep your end goal in mind if you are going to stay sane during your immigration case.

Some days you might feel like you've been waiting FOREVER for that decision letter to arrive. Sometimes you may feel frustrated or nervous. There may be sacrifices you will make to pay government and legal fees.

These are the days when you need to repeat this mantra to yourself:

It's not easy, but it's worth it!

You might think I'm joking or exaggerating the challenges, but I'm really not. I've been on this journey with many couples before. But don't give up... (just kidding, I knew you weren't going to do that!) ... your long-term vision for your life as a couple will provide the strength and tenacity you need to get this done.

I've written this book to answer your burning questions and give you the information you need to feel knowledgeable and prepared.

So let's get down to business...

What?! No Automatic Green Card?

Section 2

The #1 immigration urban legend of all time

Most Americans "know" that all an immigrant has to do to get a green card is marry a U.S. citizen, right?

That is to say... most Americans except for the ones who have actually gotten green cards for their foreign spouses!

If you are just getting started on your marriage immigration journey, your preliminary Google searches have probably dashed some of your preconceived notions that getting the green card was going to be fast, quick, or easy.

It's true that marrying a citizen is one potential way for some immigrants to become permanent residents of the U.S. However, even for those who qualify there are numerous bureaucratic hoops that may take months or even years to jump through correctly.

And unfortunately, for some immigrant spouses of U.S. citizens, there simply is no legal way for them to become permanent residents of the U.S.

That's why I consider the "automatic green card" idea to be the #1 immigration urban legend – it's just not true.

❤ ❤ ❤

A snapshot of the journey ahead

So now that we've debunked the biggest immigration urban legend, let's talk about reality.

If you've been looking into this at all, you have probably heard or read many things about how it all works.

You've also probably noticed that some of the things you've heard seem contradictory. That may be because different couples have different paths they must take to get to the green card. (By the way, another reason what you read seems contradictory is that you can't believe everything you find on the internet!)

I want to break down for you the main legal paths that exist for spouses of American citizens to get permanent residence (aka, a green card).

There are, of course, other more obscure and complex paths that some couples must take, but those are the sorts of things that nerdy lawyers like me to strategize about and debate amongst each other.

I promise you that these cases of legal gymnastics are not something you actually want to read about in this book!

When breaking down the most common paths to a green card, I think it's best to start by talking about the different situations a couple might find themselves in at the point where they are engaged or married:

- They might both currently live in the U.S.

- They might both live in a foreign country

- The foreign partner might live abroad and the American might live in the U.S.

- The foreign partner might live abroad but temporarily be physically together at the moment with the American in the U.S. (for example, on a tourist visa, a student visa, etc.).

Depending on which of these situations the couple is in, they will need to take a different path.

♥ ♥ ♥

So what are the different paths available? Let's go through the most common ones now. Keep in mind that this is over-simplified, general information. So don't make any decisions or file any paperwork based on this information alone!

Path 1: Adjustment of Status

"Adjustment of status" is the technical term for the process where an immigrant who is in the U.S. switches from a temporary status (like a visitor's or student visa) to having a green card.

Many couples prefer to do an adjustment of status if they qualify, because it is done at a U.S. Citizenship and Immigration Services (USCIS) office inside of the United States, and can be done all in one step.

Path 2: Fiancé Visa + Adjustment of Status

If the couple is only engaged (not yet legally married), and the foreign fiancé is abroad, the American can apply for a fiancé visa so that the immigrant can travel into the U.S.

After the fiancé arrives, the couple gets married in the U.S., and then does an adjustment of status.

Path 3: Petition + Consular Processing

What if the couple is already married and the foreign spouse is abroad? A fiancé visa is only available for an unmarried couple, so that option doesn't work. However, the American spouse can do a spouse petition and go through "consular processing" in a U.S. embassy abroad. This option will enable the foreign spouse to enter the U.S. directly as a permanent resident.

Keep in mind that sometimes certain details of the foreign partner's history (immigration, criminal, medical and more) can cause difficulties with one or more of these pathways. Sometimes even the past actions of the American partner cause problems, as strange as that sounds.

Problems with either partner's history can in some cases be overcome with waivers or other legal maneuvers. I mention this now just so you are aware of this and make sure to get good advice about your own situation. Don't start any legal process unless you know for sure that you qualify.

Eenie-meenie-miny-moh: choosing which path to take

So now you have an idea of the main pathways used by most married couples to get a green card:

- Adjustment of Status
- Fiancé Visa
- Consular Processing

But how does each couple choose what option to use?

The choice is partly based on what the couple legally qualifies to do, and partly based on their person preferences.

Let's go through the most important factors that usually play a role in this decision for any couple.

❤ ❤ ❤

Adjustment of Status

Who qualifies?

There are a lot of legal rules about who is able to adjust status. Immigrants who have entered the U.S. with a valid visa and have never done anything to violate the conditions of their visa may qualify to go through this process.

However, there are some important exceptions to this rule.

For example, if the immigrant has a J-1 Visa (issued to some students), they may be required to leave the U.S. for two years before returning for a green card, even if they are married to a U.S. citizen. (Arg – this is another example of how much of a myth it is that marrying a citizen solves all your immigration problems!)

Another example of an exception is if the immigrant entered on a fiancé visa, but later married a DIFFERENT American than the one who applied for the fiancé visa. That isn't allowed.

Another tricky area where adjustment of status problems come up is in cases in which USCIS believes the immigrant came to the U.S. with a temporary visa (like a tourist visa, for example), but at the time they actually planned to get married and adjust status. This is also not allowed.

If a couple got married very soon after the immigrant came to the U.S. on any type of visa other than a fiancé visa, it can cause major problems.

Keep in mind that there are some immigrants who did not enter with a valid visa or who entered with a valid visa but violated the conditions of the visa, but they STILL qualify to adjust their status.

These exceptions can involve some serious legal gymnastics such as invoking old laws based on a petition filed for the immigrant or the immigrant's parents decades ago, or using a humanitarian program in creative ways to make the immigrant adjustment-eligible.

But PLEASE don't try any of those without a lawyer's help!

No matter what your situation, you need to be extra, extra sure that your case qualifies for adjustment of status before you file any paperwork! (Hint: this quick overview is NOT enough information for you to know definitively whether you qualify.)

Pros of Adjustment of Status:

- It is done without having to travel abroad
- It tends to be the fastest type of marriage green card case
- The paperwork can be sent in all at one time

Cons of Adjustment of Status:

- A lot of couples don't qualify
- If USCIS thinks you used a tourist visa planning to come to the U.S. and adjust status, they can deny your case (or even accuse you of fraud, eek!)
- The immigrant can't leave the U.S. after filing the case, unless a special travel permit is obtained. But just getting a travel permit takes months. So for immigrants who travel abroad frequently, adjustment of status might not be a good fit.

♥ ♥ ♥

Fiancé Visa

Who qualifies?

Unmarried couples where the foreign fiancé lives in another country sometimes qualify for this. They usually have to have met each other in person at least one time in the two years before they apply for the fiancé visa, and they have to plan on getting married in the U.S. within 90 days of the immigrant arriving.

After coming to the U.S. on the fiancé visa and getting married, the couple then goes through the adjustment of status process to actually get the green card.

Pros of a Fiancé Visa:

- For unmarried couples living in different countries, the fiancé visa is usually the fastest way for them to physically be together, which is the biggest priority for many couples.
- If the couple wants to get married in the U.S. rather than in the foreign country, this is typically the best way to do it unless the immigrant is already in the U.S. on a different type of visa.
- Having up to 90 days to get married allows a couple to spend time together and make 100% sure they do want to make a marriage commitment before performing the ceremony.

Cons of a Fiancé Visa:

- If you are already married, this is not an option available to you.
- If you want to be married abroad, this is not an option for you.
- The immigrant is only able to enter the U.S. one time with a fiancé visa, so he or she can't travel abroad while on the fiancé visa or at the beginning of the adjustment of status process after the marriage.
- Having less than 90 days to get married can be stressful and complicated, especially if the wedding is going to have lots of guests.
- The fiancé visa has extra paperwork since it is a two-step process: first you have to get the fiancé visa and then you still have to adjust status.
- Even if the couple gets married and files for adjustment literally the day the fiancé arrives in the U.S., they still won't be able to work legally until they get work authorization card (usually in 90 days). If they get married and file the adjustment closer to the end of their 90-day window, the foreign spouse may not be able to work for about 6 months!

Consular Processing for an Immigrant Visa

Who qualifies?

The couple has to be legally married to do this process. This option is usually used by couples who were married abroad and now want to relocate to the U.S.

In some cases, the couple might start this process instead of adjustment of status simply because they know the foreign spouse has to go back home or travel internationally in the next few months and can't stay put long enough to do an adjustment.

Pros of Consular Processing:

- Allows the immigrant to travel internationally during the application process

- The immigrant comes to the U.S. as a legal resident, without having to take other immediate legal steps.

- The American spouse can be abroad with the foreign spouse and move back to the U.S. together after the case is won.

Cons of Consular Processing:

- To apply, most couples have to get married abroad. (This is only a drawback if you have your heart set on a wedding in the U.S.!)

- If the American partner is in the U.S., choosing marriage abroad and consular processing instead of a fiancé visa and marriage in the U.S. usually means a slightly longer separation until the couple can be together in the U.S.

- After the couple is married, but while the Immigrant Visa case is pending, the foreign partner may face additional hurdles if they try to obtain another type of visa. For example, they might want a tourist visa to visit their spouse in the U.S. The reason the tourist visa would be harder to get is that the Consulate will likely suspect that they want a tourist visa so they can go to the U.S. and adjust status, which isn't allowed.

♥ ♥ ♥

How Thinking Ahead Makes Things 300% Easier

(Approximately)

Section 3

5 Things to Start Saving Right Now

Green card cases are one of those big projects that tend to go a lot smoother if you start it off on the right foot.

You know how it takes a LONG time to find something you stuck somewhere not thinking you would need it and later you realize you do?

And you know how easy it is to find something you knew was important and set aside in a designated location ahead of time?

Preparing for an immigration case is no different. Couples who only start thinking about what documents are needed AFTER their lawyer hands them a list will have to do a lot more digging to do than those who planned on it since they were dating or engaged.

So I'm going to tell you right now what things you should be setting aside starting today! Decorate a shoebox or add a folder to your file cabinet titled "Immigration Stuff". Whenever you come across something on this list, stick it in there. You will be SO happy you did, I promise. And if you are already married? Better late than never! Get going on this asap.

❤ ❤ ❤

Here are the key things to add to your stash:

Proof you like each other:

That's right, get some of the mushy stuff: anniversary cards, love notes, photos of you doing something romantic, screenshots of cute text messages or Facebook posts about each other.

Proof you spend time together:

Save ticket stubs, party invites, and photos of you two doing all different types of activities together. If you have a long-distance relationship, save cell phone bills showing you call each other day or a few screenshots of your Skype conversations. Save your plane tickets or other proof of travel to see each other.

Proof that everybody knows you're a couple:

Cards addressed to you as a couple, photos of you with each other's parents and friends. Your love should be public knowledge, and you'll want the evidence to show that.

Originals of important documents:

Did you lose your driver's license? Is your passport expired? Is your original birth certificate in a storage unit or your parents' basement? Now is the time to make sure you have original, unexpired personal documents of all kinds.

When ordering birth certificates, marriage licenses, divorce decrees from prior marriages, etc., get 3 copies just to be safe. It's a lot easier to get multiple copies at the same time at the beginning than to get another set on short notice when the shipping company accidently sends your package to the wrong continent. (Yes, it has happened to clients of mine before!)

Proof of wedding planning:

Have you bought rings? Picked colors? Gotten your dress? Receipts, insurance policies, and other planning stuff is great to save.

♥ ♥ ♥

Disclaimer: Please do everything in MODERATION. I'm not trying to turn you into a hoarder! A handful of things from different time periods throughout your relationship in each of these categories will be enough to be in good shape once it's application time.

Key actions USCIS thinks "real" couples take

You will quickly realize through the immigration process that the government has a somewhat fixed idea of what a real relationship looks like.

It's not fair, it's not politically correct, and it's not how the modern American relationship really works. But do you want to be right or do you want a green card?!?

I would never suggest you take any particular actions solely for the sake of your immigration case. However, you need to keep USCIS's views about marriage in mind as you are working out the logistics of your relationship.

For many couples, the timing of taking different steps to join your lives and your personal paperwork together may change because of the case.

Note also that taking these actions could have serious ramifications in the case of a divorce or separation, so you might want to get legal or financial advice about what these actions might mean for you before you take them.

It is precisely the high level of risk in letting another person have control of serious parts of your life that convinces Immigration that you really trust this person and have a romantic relationship!

❤ ❤ ❤

So here is what USCIS thinks happens in a "real" marriage:

You join your finances

That usually means you have a joint checking account that you pay your regular bills from.

You live together

I'm betting this one is okay with you! Most of my clients want to be living with each other as fast as possible, if they aren't already.

On the other hand, sometimes life intervenes and due to school, family, or career issues they may have to live in different places for a while. In these cases it is important to show the "why" behind your situation. Get good help if this applies to you.

You own joint property

Married people buy houses together, cars together, and appliances together, right? This is one area where modern couples tend to have totally different arrangements depending on the couple. If in the past you two have tended to own things separately, it might be worth it to buy your next major purchase under both names.

You list each other on assets and insurance policies

This means joint medical, home, and auto policies. You list each other as beneficiaries of each other's life insurance and investment accounts.

Are you toast if you don't exactly fit with this description? Of course not! USCIS looks at your relationship as a whole when deciding whether it is legit. But you better have other good evidence to make up for any shortcomings in your case.

❤ ❤ ❤

Do I have to change my last name?

Considering USCIS's traditional idea of marriage, many women ask me whether they have to change their last name when they get married.

It's a great question, but luckily this is one area that USCIS is not going to get into your personal business. So make the decision based on your own preference.

Some women want to change their names and some don't. Sure, if you change your name and use your married name publicly it is additional evidence that the relationship is real. However, not changing your name doesn't prove that the relationship is not real!

Changing your name can have ramifications as far as your career, personal and cultural identity, and more, so don't feel pressured to do it if you are not inclined to. Whew.

To make this personal decision, do some soul-searching: Would you change your name if there were no immigration case to be filed? That should be the only question you ask yourself.

❤ ❤ ❤

Timing is Everything

Section 4

Crystal balls and other ways to guess how long it will take

So how long will my case take?"

This is one of the first questions my clients ask me, and is really a tough one to answer.

The truth is that no one truly knows. Timing is one of the most unpredictable things about an immigration case.

Timing is also one of the hardest things to deal with on an emotional level. Why is that?

Although there are general timeframes for different case types, there are also many factors out of your control that can cause your case to take significantly longer:

- Government requests for more documents (which unfortunately can happen even if all of the requirements are sent from the beginning)
- Delays because of an increase in applications filed by other applicants
- Changes in government procedures in the middle of your case
- Technology problems
- Mail problems
- Difficulty obtaining necessary documents

It can be frustrating to know that so many of these factors are out of your control. However, many of the most common factors that cause a case to take longer actually ARE under your control!

If you want to finish as soon as possible, be sure to:

- Hire your immigration lawyer as soon as possible so you can get to work asap
- Collect your personal and relationship documents quickly
- Stay in contact with your lawyer and assigned paralegal, and respond to any of their requests as soon as possible
- Wear your lucky socks daily or maintain the performance of your other preferred superstitions (Haha, just kidding!)

There are also a few ways that you can keep tabs on your case as it makes its way through the system.

The tricky thing about tracking your immigration case online is that, depending on the type of case you have, it may go through different offices inside of the United States and with the Department of State abroad. And some of these offices assign you a new case number when they take over the case!

Tracking with USCIS

For some phases in a case with USCIS, there is a form that your lawyer can file so you get an email or text message when the case is received.

You will also get a receipt notice by mail showing your assigned case number, which you can use to check up on your case electronically.

During the time the case is with U.S. Citizenship and Immigration Services (USCIS), you can get status information at www.uscis.gov. You can even sign up for direct notifications by email when the status changes.

USCIS also has current average processing times for certain case types posted on the website. That can give you a good ballpark estimate of the timeframe.

Keep in mind that these estimates are only for the phase of the process while the case is with USCIS, so it doesn't take into account the subsequent steps your case may have to go through. Also, this is an average, so it doesn't take into account some of the random things that might happen in your particular case.

Tracking with the NVC

If part of your process involves the National Visa Center (NVC), a new case number will be assigned along with an invoice ID. The NVC has an online system where you can see which parts of their process have been submitted and what still needs done.

Cases that go the Department of State are held at the individual US Consulate in the foreign country where the case is being processed, and there is an electronic system for selecting interview dates.

These different offices can also be contacted directly by phone and email. However, your attorney should be the one to check up on your case, and he or she will probably only do so if it seems like something unusual is going on. The last thing you would want to do is cause a delay because of your inquiries!

Tracking with the Department of State

Okay, so maybe "tracking" is not exactly the right word in the case of the DOS. You can, however, check their website for current interview wait times by location so you can get an idea.

❤ ❤ ❤

There is no doubt that the wait can be excruciating, especially if you are far apart from your sweetie while you wait, but hang in there!

It is important to have a plan of action ahead of time about how you will cope with the wait.

You know yourself better than anyone else, so make a list of strategies that work for you in times of stress. You can use our worksheet on the next page to help you figure this out.

Have your plan handy for days when you need it. Or even better, start some self-care routines now so that there are fewer of those tough days to get through.

My "Happy Healthy" Worksheet

Here are some things that help me stay healthy and happy (Circle all that apply, including new things you'd like to try):

Take a walk	**Do yard work**
Bubble Bath	**Clean/Organize things**
Go to a park	**Dance**
Gratitude Practice	**Play with kids**
Follow a blog	**Netflix binge**
Get a massage	**Manicure/pedicure**
Be in nature	**Fresh flowers**
Meditate	**Go running**
Pray	**Good-smelling lotion**
Work out	**Talk with a friend**
Go rock climbing	**Funny movies**
Go hiking	**Girls' Night**
Yoga	**Other: _____**
Go for a drive	

People who can remind me to do something on this list when I get stressed out:

_____   _____

My immigration motto (pick one or write one):

☐ It isn't easy, but it's worth it

☐ This too shall pass

☐ _____

Now write down your motto somewhere you can refer to it as needed!

Tips for planning a timeline-neutral wedding

Planning a wedding is tough enough as it is. Once you add in immigration requirements and timelines to the mix, it really gets complicated.

But it can be done! Here are some tips on how to pull it off when you can't pick an exact date far in advance like most brides traditionally do.

- Choose a venue that you don't have to reserve far in advance (a family or friend's home or backyard works well). Or choose a few places that sometimes have last minute openings and be prepared to call them all once you have the exact date.

- Make or buy decorations that can be stored until needed. For example, do candles instead of flowers.

- Get things "mostly done", such as having everything set up for your invitations and ready to be printed as soon as the date is known.

- Vet multiple vendors for each category of your needs (photographer, musician, cake decorator, etc, so you can have a list of potential options to call once you know the date.)

- Find out what the marriage license requirements are in your county ahead of time so you can get one asap once you're ready.

- For an officiant, you can use a company that has access to many officiants to make sure someone will be available on your chosen day.

Also remember it is perfectly fine to have a legal wedding first and the wedding of your dreams later on! That is a popular option for many couples for logistical reasons.

Just be sure you talk with your lawyer ahead of time about how to best present the details of your wedding in your application so you don't raise any red flags with immigration.

❤ ❤ ❤

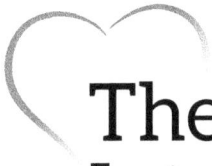

The Marriage Interview

Section 5

Debunking Top Internet Rumors about the Marriage Interview

Ah, the internet. It is so wonderful, yet at the same time the source of so much anxiety about the immigration process...

I know you don't need me to tell you not to believe everything you read online. Obviously.

And I know you have a carefully honed BS detector you've developed over years of Googling stuff.

But the tricky thing about online research on immigration law is that it's actually pretty hard to tell what is true and what's not. If I weren't an immigration lawyer, I wouldn't be able to tell it apart either.

Why?

First, I think part of the problem is that each individual immigrant's situation is so unique that it is almost impossible to tell whether any particular thing that happened to someone else would apply in your case.

It is fairly common for clients to tell me about their friend whose case is "exactly" the same as theirs. This usually comes up when the client is hoping that they qualify for options other than the ones I've presented. Or sometimes they are worried about something they have heard about that turns out to not even apply in their case.

The thing is that nobody's life is exactly the same as anybody else's is. It might seem like all the main, important things are the same... but our immigration system is unfortunately fairly illogical and sometimes makes weird, picky distinctions that make a big difference in the outcome.

Plus, immigration law changes a lot, and very quickly. There are tons of people out there who legitimately received green cards through processes that are no longer available today.

And unfortunately, there are also other people out there who think they have no options because they previously consulted with a lawyer... but don't realize that the law has changed in their favor since then.

If you add these factors onto the natural internet "telephone" effect of things being repeated over and over again in a slightly different way, it is no wonder why it is so hard to make sense of it.

The moral of this story is:

The only way you can be sure something applies to you or not is if you've recently consulted an immigration lawyer who works frequently with your type of situation. (And maybe you've even gotten a second opinion.)

❤ ❤ ❤

Okay, now that we've gotten that out of the way, here are some of the top internet rumors you might have heard:

RUMOR: They ask you about your sex life at the interview.

REALITY: This has never happened to any of my clients or to the clients of any lawyers I know. I'm not going to say it has never happened in the history of the world, but it is definitely not common at all. If an officer were to start asking questions like this at an interview, your lawyer would probably intervene.

RUMOR: You will "fail" the interview if you don't get every question right.

REALITY: No couple knows everything about each other, and every person's perception of reality is different. If your answers matched up perfectly, it actually might look suspicious. During the interview, if you are asked something that you don't know or can't remember, just say so.

RUMOR: The interview is no big deal, so don't worry about it.

REALITY: The interview is really important, and is a key part of getting your application approved. Don't freak out about it, but do prepare ahead of time. Also, don't get too comfortable with the officer or joke around. Be professional. Answer the questions, but don't volunteer extra information.

There is a tendency by people who have already been approved to say it was no big deal. But remember they are saying that after their case was meticulously prepared and they went into the interview in the right frame of mind. It is easy to later forget all of the preparation you did ahead of time, so the interview seemed less intimidating.

RUMOR: The questions and answers are the only thing that matters for the officer to make a decision about the interview.

REALITY: The interview answers make up just one part of the officer's decision about whether your relationship is legitimate. Officers also do research on the couple ahead of time, both based on the application submitted and other things they are able to find out. Believe me, they already know things like whether or not your mail goes to the same address and if anyone else lives there.

♥ ♥ ♥

Debunking Top Internet Rumors about the Marriage Interview

Everyone wants to know what USCIS is really looking for when they decide whether to approve or deny a marriage application. Fortunately, immigration lawyers around the country have been working hard to discover every possible inside detail about the process to use for the advantage of our clients.

A few years ago, the American Immigration Lawyers Association (also known as "AILA") obtained an internal USCIS document titled "Fraud Referral Sheet" that lists what they consider to be red flags in applications.

In other words, if any of these factors apply to you and your significant other, your relationship may face additional scrutiny during the process:

- Date of prior divorce and current marriage are close together
- Large age difference between spouses
- Short time between entry into the U.S. and marriage
- Both spouses work for the same employer
- Unusual cultural differences (language, religion, etc.)
- Unusual marriage history (quick wedding, many previous marriages, marrying right before visa expires, etc.)
- The American spouse was previously married to other foreigners and/or has filed petitions before
- The foreign spouse has previously been petitioned for by another American
- One spouse has had a child with someone else during the current marriage

Some of the other red flags listed in the USCIS document have to do not with the couple's relationship or history, but with who prepared the application and how well (or poorly) it was done:

- Evidence presented was obtained just before or immediately after the interview

- Too much evidence is submitted (an "over-submission")

- Documents look suspicious

- Photos look staged

- Tax filing or financial transactions are suspicious

- The application was done by an attorney or document preparer ("notario") that the government already suspects is involved in fraud

- The same individual prepared the documents and notarized other documents or performed the wedding

There are also some types of behavior during the interview that will make USCIS suspicious:

- Extreme nervousness, over-interaction, lack of knowledge about basic questions, lack of interest or interaction with significant other, no eye contact, evasive or general answers, or arrived late for the interview

- Unusual behavior by attorney, interpreter, or other spouse during the interview: prompts answers, interrupts other person during answers, or attempts to distract or mislead

♥ ♥ ♥

An insider's compilation of the classic questions

So what types of questions do they ask at the marriage interview, anyway? The marriage interview is the stuff that movies (and internet urban legends) are made of.

In real life interviews, there tend to be certain categories of questions that are asked most frequently.

To satisfy your curiosity, here's a list of those typical categories and some examples for each:

Questions about Biographical Info of Spouse

- Where was your spouse born?
- What country is your spouse from?
- Are your spouse's parents living or deceased? What are their names?
- How many siblings does your spouse have? What are their names? Where do they live?
- Does your spouse have any children?
- Has your spouse ever been married before?
- When did your spouse first come to the United States?

Questions about the Relationship

- When did you meet?
- How did you meet?
- How long did you know each other before you started dating?
- When did you first meet each other's families?
- When did you get engaged?
- Was there a proposal?
- How long were you engaged before you got married?
- What day did you get married?
- Did you get married at the courthouse or in a religious ceremony?
- Who attended your wedding?
- Was your spouse's family at the wedding? Was your family there?
- How many people attended the wedding? The reception?
- Where was the reception?

So what types of questions do they ask at the marriage interview, anyway? The marriage interview is the stuff that movies (and internet urban legends) are made of.

In real life interviews, there tend to be certain categories of questions that are asked most frequently.

To satisfy your curiosity, here's a list of those typical categories and some examples for each:

Questions about Biographical Info of Spouse

- Where was your spouse born?
- What country is your spouse from?
- Are your spouse's parents living or deceased? What are their names?
- How many siblings does your spouse have? What are their names? Where do they live?
- Does your spouse have any children?
- Has your spouse ever been married before?
- When did your spouse first come to the United States?

Questions about the Relationship

- When did you meet?
- How did you meet?
- How long did you know each other before you started dating?
- When did you first meet each other's families?
- When did you get engaged?
- Was there a proposal?
- How long were you engaged before you got married?
- What day did you get married?
- Did you get married at the courthouse or in a religious ceremony?
- Who attended your wedding?
- Was your spouse's family at the wedding? Was your family there?
- How many people attended the wedding? The reception?
- Where was the reception?

Questions about Daily Habits

- What time does your spouse wake up in the morning?

- Which of you gets out of bed first?
- What time do you each go to bed?
- Does your spouse eat breakfast before going to work?
- What is your spouse's normal work schedule?
- How long is his/her commute to work?
- Where do you each plug in your cell phones to charge?
- How many bedrooms are there in your house/apartment?

Questions about Celebrations

- How did you celebrate:
- Your spouse's birthday
- Valentine's Day
- Christmas
- New Years' Eve
- 4th of July, etc.
- Do you plan on taking any vacations this year?
- When was the last time you visited his/her family?
- Have his/her relatives ever visited you at your house?

Questions if the Couple is Expecting a Baby

- How far along is the pregnancy?
- Is it a boy or girl?
- What is the obstetrician's name?
- Have you decided on a name?
- Where will the baby be sleeping?
- Who will take care of the baby once it's born?
- How much time do you each plan to take off?

Remember that the questions you are asked won't necessarily be the ones listed here. Each officer asks different questions to different couples. However, this list hopefully gives you a general idea of what to expect.

What's Next?

Section 6

How to choose your lawyer

As soon as you are engaged (or asap, if you're already married), one of the first steps you should take is to select the immigration lawyer you will be working with. Your lawyer will advise you from the very beginning about the specific steps in your case and what types of evidence will be needed.

You might be wondering WHY your choice of lawyer matters —aren't all lawyers the same?

I thought the very same thing many years ago when I first looked for an immigration lawyer to help me and my husband with his case, which was years before I became a lawyer myself.

It wasn't until we went to a few consultations that we realized finding a lawyer would be more complicated than we thought (one lawyer we saw was rude to us, one didn't want to help us at all, and one talked over our heads).

Unfortunately, these first three lawyers also gave us what turned out to be terrible legal advice... and as a result my husband ended up stuck in Guatemala while our baby daughter was with me in the United States battling leukemia.

It was not until we found an excellent immigration lawyer that the whole mess got straightened out.

Today my husband is a U.S. citizen, and our daughter is healthy. And after this experience, I became an immigration lawyer and started a law firm to help couples who find themselves in the same situation that we once were in.

So yes, the choice of lawyer matters! My husband would not be

a citizen and we would not be living in the United States right now if not for the work of our lawyer (who is now retired).

But how can you find a good lawyer? I'll admit that it's hard to tell the difference between an excellent lawyer and a bad or mediocre one, but here is a good place to start:

✔ Make sure the "lawyer" is actually a lawyer. In most states there is a list of all licensed lawyers on the state government website and whether or not they have been disciplined. Just remember that some immigration lawyers are licensed in a state other than where they currently live, so don't jump to any conclusions if you don't see their name on the list! If in doubt, ask what state they are licensed in and check up on it.

✔ Make sure the lawyer only practices immigration law and nothing else. Immigration is complicated enough that lawyers don't have the time to keep up on all of the latest developments unless they only do immigration.

✔ Pick an immigration lawyer whose practice focuses on couples. For example, you wouldn't be best served in your marriage case by an immigration lawyer who mostly does asylum or mostly helps large companies bring in skilled workers, or any of the other sub-niches in immigration law.

✔ Pick a lawyer you feel fundamentally comfortable with. If you have a gut feeling that they don't have your best interest mind, go see someone else.

✔ Ask other couples you know who they have worked with for their case and whether they were satisfied.

✔ Check online reviews of the lawyer you are considering. Of course, take these with a grain of salt because not everything you read on the internet is true!

♥ ♥ ♥

One other question that many couples have is whether they even need legal representation. Is an immigration case the sort of thing a person can do themselves guided by some online tips?

I tend to think that everyone should use a lawyer (or a non-profit organization that is BIA accredited, if they can't afford a lawyer). But that is just because I've had a lot of people hire me after things went horribly wrong for them without a lawyer!

This is really a question you have to ask yourself, and the answer will be personal. Your answer will likely depend on how important it is to you to win your case and how much risk you can tolerate.

Here are some questions that may be helpful to reflect on together as you weigh your options:

- Do we prefer to live in the United States instead of abroad? Why?

- If we lived abroad, how different would our lives be in terms of jobs, opportunities, education, safety, relationship to friends and family, and raising a family?

- How important is it to us that we live in the United States?

- What would happen in our lives and marriage if we did not successfully get a green card?

- Would we or would we not be stressed out sending in applications we are not sure are right? How about going to an interview alone without being sure of exactly sure what to expect?

- How important is it to get this done as soon as possible? Will it be a problem for us if our case is delayed by several months or even years because everything was not submitted correctly the first time?

- How much does it cost us financially for each month that the foreign spouse is not able to legally work in the United States?

- How much money are we spending to maintain separate households in different countries and fly back and forth to see each other?

- How will the stress of the case and time commitment involved affect our relationship?

No matter what you decide to do or which lawyer you pick, the important thing is to take your first step to start moving forward. If you don't start, you won't ever get to your happily ever after!

♥ ♥ ♥

Best Wishes

It's been a pleasure talking about immigration law with you! I'm excited for you and all that lies ahead.

I wish you the best on your journey and hope that in the near future your spouse will become one of our country's newest permanent residents.

Take care,

Clm Cond

Bonus Material

**"Immigration for Couples"
seminar transcripts**

Part 1 - Marriage Immigration Options 101

Megan: Good evening everyone. We're going to go ahead and get started. Thank you so much for joining us. Welcome to Part 1 of the seminar series "Immigration for Couples". Marriage Immigration Options 101. My name's Megan and I'll be hosting tonight's call with immigration attorney Clare Corado. Clare is the founder of the law firm Corado Immigration Law, which is dedicated to helping Americans get citizenship for their foreign spouses.

    This is the first in a series of 5 seminars. We hope to be able to send all of you the links to our 5 seminars shortly after that date so you can listen to them again or listen to her recording that you may have missed. Also, Clare will be staying on for a question and answer session tonight at the end of this seminar so please stick around for that.

    Clare, are you ready to get started?

Clare: Yes, I am. Thank you Megan. I'm really excited to talk about tonight's topic: the different immigration options for people who are hoping to get permanent residence, also known as a green card, through a marriage. I do have a little bit of a cough so I'm going to try not to cough too much. I have my water here with me.

    I also wanted to mention that if for some reason my call drops I'm just going to call right back in. I tried to think of somebody who had a land line I could call from and I just couldn't think of anybody. If that happens just hang on for a second, I'll be back on the line. The same with any of you. If your call drops for whatever reason you can call back the same conference number that you called in on and use your pass code and you'll just come right back into the call.

    For those of you who are out there just starting out on your immigration journey, I know we find a lot of our clients really just want as much information as possible to get a good idea of what they're getting into at the beginning. I think that's great. It's great to go into everything with your eyes open and have a good idea of what to expect. It's a really exciting time in your life if you're getting married or you recently got married. Congratulations on that! Whenever you're marrying someone who's from a foreign country, you always have that added element of dealing with the immigration side of things so that you can settle down and form your lives together here in the United States.

A lot of my clients, when they start researching they're in the information gathering stage. They get on Google and they're reading a whole bunch of stuff. Google can be a great starting point, but what I find is that people start to really get confused and get some conflicting information and, honestly, get scared because they're reading lots of crazy things that are online. Some of them are just completely inaccurate. Some of them are accurate in certain situations, but they don't apply to that person at all. That's kind of the tricky thing about Google. We've created this seminar because we saw such a need for getting some good information out there and having people ask some questions about the things that we're talking about, too.

One thing I did want to say before we get started though is that we're going to give you some information so you have a better idea of what the process might entail in your case. These calls are not going to be a good substitute for a personal consultation with a good immigration lawyer. This is kind of just the starting point. I do believe we actually even have some other lawyers and some law students on the line, which is exciting. Some people on here might just be interested in the topic and not even have a personal case. We're happy to see you on the line as well.

Before you would ever file anything or move forward we definitely recommend that you talk with someone, a licensed attorney who you're sure is really an attorney, and someone who does 100% immigration law and works with married and engaged couples. That definitely would be my recommendation.

Let's jump right into the topic then. We're going to talk about the different types of options for couples who are looking to go through an immigration process through their marriage. There are a few different main options. A lot of people are very surprised when they start the Googling process. They think that there's going to be one way that it's done. They think, "We start by doing this. There's something called a petition that we heard about and then we end up with a green card." There are actually a few different ways that it's done. Depending on your situation you would use a different approach. Today we're going to talk about the most common ones, but there are other ways too that are less common. We're not going to get into the really crazy stuff. That's the sort of thing that nerdy immigration lawyers like to talk about, but you probably don't want to hear about it in a general conference.

The sort of factors that would affect what option would be appropriate for you would be things like what country is your fiancé or spouse from? Is your fiancé or spouse physically in the United States right now or are they in a country abroad? Whether the American, whoever is the American relationship or the resident, whether they are physically in the United States and where their residence is. You might be an American living abroad, and that would affect how it was approached as well.

Another thing that's really important is going to be your future plans as a couple. Even starting with the wedding and then from there on. Are you wanting to get married in the United States? Do you want to get married abroad? How soon do you want to be in the United States, and do you have a certain time frame? Those factors can be really important as far as what options are going to be best for you.

The first general situation that we see, or general option, would be when the American is inside the United States and the fiancé is abroad, and they want to get married inside the United States. This option is commonly referred to as a fiancé visa or a K-1. The basic process is that you get the person to come into the United States on this temporary type of visa which basically gives them permission to be able to get married here inside the United States and then continue the green card process inside the United States. We'll get into more details here in a few minutes about the basic process. First of all, let's talk about the requirements for a fiancé visa. Just the general requirements.

First of all, you have to be a fiancé. You can't be already married. If you're already married, this would be an option that you would have to discard immediately. There are other things that would be more appropriate in your case. Next, you have to be legally able to marry. This is something people sometimes overlook, but if you haven't finalized a divorce yet or there's some other problem with being legally married in the United States, for example, if you're going to get married in a state that does not allow cousins to marry each other and you're actually related or for any reason you wouldn't be legally able to get married inside the United States, then you wouldn't be able to qualify for a fiancé visa either.

You must have met your fiancé in person at least once in the 2 years before you apply for the fiancé visa. For popular culture there's the stereotype that people will meet online, they've never met and they bring their fiancé over and they're meeting for the first time at their wedding, or something like that. That actually isn't possible. There are some exceptions to that rule of having to have met in person, but they're very strict and they're usually religious reasons where it would just be totally inappropriate in your culture to have even seen each other in person before the wedding. That's not something we see very often.

You have to have the intention to get married within 90 days of coming into the United States. That one's not particularly difficult to meet the requirement as far as proving it. Usually we submit a statement literally saying, "I intend to get married within 90 days of entry," and then submit proof of your relationship and that you actually are engaged and planning to get married.

The American actually has some requirements as far as their criminal history. Usually in immigration cases the American family member's history is not really involved in the case. However, with K-1 visas, there are rules about petitioners, you're limited in your ability petition if you have certain types of crimes in your past mostly having to do with child abuse and things like that. I guess there have historically been some problems with that. People actually petitioning for their fiancés abroad and bringing them and their children over and maybe that person could actually harm those people. At least there was a fear of it. I'm not really sure how much that actually happened. They've taken some steps to prevent that from happening. If the American has any sort of history that might bump up against that possibility at all that's definitely something you want to talk with an attorney about and get checked out pretty thoroughly because that requirement does exist too.

There are a lot of different problems that can disqualify the foreign fiancé. In immigration law those are called "grounds of inadmissibility." We're going to talk in a lot more detail about those on a future call. I did want to mention though that even if you meet all these requirements we're talking about today, there can still be things that would prevent you from actually being able to get a fiancé visa or from being able to get a green card through your marriage. If you're interested in that, and I hope you are because it's a very important part of the topic, definitely make sure you don't miss that class or listen to the recording once we have those out.

The basic process for the fiancé visa option is first of all that you do a petition. The American has to show that they meet all those requirements that I just mentioned, that both people intend to marry each other, that they've met in person, that they are legally able to marry. All those requirements. That application goes to an office here in the United States and they hopefully approve it. Sometimes they might ask for more evidence. It can kind of get stalled in any of the different offices just because it's a very bureaucratic process. Once that petition gets approved and they say, "Okay, we agree that it looks like you really want to marry this person and you meet the requirements for the fiancé visa," they will send that through an intermediary office. I really don't know why because it seems like they could just send it directly somewhere. It'd be a lot faster.

It does go through another office and eventually arrives at the US embassy in your fiancé's country, or in some cases in the country where your fiancé would apply. In most cases in your fiancé's country there will be a US embassy where they'll actually receive the visa.

Once the approved petition arrives at that embassy, each embassy has slightly different procedures as far as how they want you to actually sign up for an interview and get different documents to them. They all involve paperwork and passing a medical exam, getting vaccines, things like that, and scheduling an interview at the embassy. If everything goes well at the embassy, it's actually called the consulate. It's a section within the embassy. One of the functions that an embassy does, they will approve the visa so it will get actually placed in the passport of the fiancé, then they can travel to the United States and get married within the 90 days.

Once question I get a lot, which I think is a great question, is how much time do you have to come to the US after you get the visa and your passport? Some people, maybe they get the visa but they have to do some other things. They have to tie up some loose ends before they can actually move to the United States. The visa will have an expiration date on it. Usually you get 6 months to go into the United States and actually use that visa. The visa is called, it's a single entry visa, which means you can only go in once as a fiancé. It's really important that when the fiancé uses that visa and goes into the United States that they follow through, assuming that they still want to, they follow through with the marriage and the entire green card process inside the United States. If they leave, they're not prevented from trying again, but they have to start back at the beginning of the process or pursue a different option. That's just something to keep in mind.

If everything goes well and they get married, then they can get a green card in the United States. Two years after that they have to go through another process called removal of conditions. That is just to make sure that they get a permanent green card basically. That's a topic we can probably get into on a different call as well, although I don't think we have that one scheduled yet. If you're interested, let me know and we'll get that scheduled.

The main things I think that are important for couples to consider when they're thinking about going the fiancé visa route is, first of all, is it important to us if we get married here in the United States or abroad? If you definitely don't want to get married in the United States or you definitely do want to get married in the United States, that could make your choice for you.

One thing I think is really important to point out, and we work with a lot of couples when they're making these important decisions, is just because you want to have the ceremony and the party in one place it doesn't necessarily mean that the legal ceremony or legal proceeding … I guess it's not a proceeding, it's a contract or something. It sounds so sad to call a marriage that, doesn't it? Legally that's what it is. You don't actually have to have the civil process in the same place. We'll have people who they decide that really the best option for them, as far as the time frame and the legal process, is going to be to get a fiancé visa but they had their heart set on having their wedding somewhere else abroad or on some Caribbean island or something. What they'll sometimes do is get the fiancé visa, come to the US, finish the green card process and then plan their wedding and their party and their friends and family and everything ceremonial out a year or something so that they can get that in their own preferred time frame.

Excuse me. I've got to drink some of my water. I warned you that might happen. Okay. Thank you.

Another thing that you really want to consider if you're considering the fiancé visa option is can the fiancé spend a few months in the United States without being able to work and not be able to travel abroad? I mentioned this a little bit earlier, once the fiancé comes into the US and they are going to get married within 90 days, then file and application called the adjustment of status that will get them the green card. They really can't work for a few months. Supposedly … It's kind of one of those silly, illogical situations that we unfortunately see in immigration law sometimes where if you look it up technically someone on a K-1, they can get work authorization. You can search that and you'll see that that's the case.

The problem is in practical reality you're really not going to get it because you have the K-1 visa, you have 90 days to be in the United States. It also takes 90 days to get work authorization. Even if you apply for work authorization the day that you get into the United States on your K-1 visa, chances are you won't have time to get it. Maybe you get it and it's immediately expired. It just doesn't make any sense at all. What we do to minimize that time without work authorization is to try to get the couple to marry at least legally, as soon as possible after the person enters, and then file or their adjustment of status so that the 90 days will start and they'll be able to get their work authorization because of their pending green card application and not because of the fiancé visa.

The problem is either way, they're probably going to spend at least 3 or 4 months in the US and not be able to work legally. For some people that's okay, but for some people it's just really a deal breaker. They need to be working in their career abroad. They're going to pursue a different option which we'll get to some of those options in a minute. That's something definitely to consider.

Another thing is it's really important when people are deciding about the fiancé visa option is timing. How quickly do we want to be able to come to the US? Right now timing varies a lot in immigration law. There are some ways to look up what the current processing times are. For immigration lawyers who do a lot of these cases, we have an idea of how long it's been taking recently and the differences that we've seen, the average case time. At least for right now, recently, the fiancé visas have been the fastest way to get someone to get the foreign part of the couple into the United States physically.

If your goal is we just want to be together as fast as we possibly can, typically we'll recommend the fiancé visa route to achieve that. That can be an important consideration as well, obviously.

Fiancé visas have a couple of more steps. Some people just don't want to deal with that much hassle and they prefer one of the more direct routes to a green card process, which we'll discuss. Some people have within their religious practice, they may feel that they are unable to travel together or be together unescorted before they're married. That can be a problem if you're coming in on a fiancé visa, even if you're not living in the same house, some people would find that inappropriate. What we sometimes advise people in that situation to do is to have a religious, but not civil, ceremony in their country abroad so that the foreign part of the couple, the foreigner, can come into the United States without that cultural problem and actually finish the process.

You'd have to be very sure that the religious wedding that was happening abroad was not legally a marriage under the law in the country where it took place. That could be a good option for people who want to be together quickly but also have that religious component problem of traveling together or of being together in the United States before the marriage was performed.

I also just wanted to mention quickly about the fiancé visas is if the fiancé has children they can usually bring them on what's called a K-2 visa. They'll go through the same process all together. That is definitely possible. We do see a lot of cases where people are going to bring their children and live with their step-parent in the United States. They do not have to be left behind, fortunately.

Just to recap, that was the option, the first option which is when the American is in the United States, the fiancé is abroad, they're not married yet and they want to get married inside the United States.

The next situation that we see is if you are already married to your foreign spouse and he or she is abroad, then you might be living abroad or you might be in the United States but you plan on living in the United States. In this case a fiancé visa would not be possible because you're already married, right? You're disqualified from doing that. That would be not good to claim you are not married. I see all kinds of crazy things honestly in this line of work, but you definitely want to always tell the truth on your applications. If you're not sure if some type of truth that you're going to tell is going to disqualify you, that's when an immigration lawyer can tell you. They'll tell you what will happen before it happens. That's a very good thing to have.

If you're married already, discard the fiancé visa option. Your options would be either a K-3 visa or what's called "consular processing." With the K-3 option, it's similar to the K-1 process where it gives you a temporary way to come into the United States and then finish the process inside of the United States. There are times when it makes sense to do the K-3 visa and times when it doesn't. It basically depends on the current processing time for the K-3 petitions.

If you remember when I was talking about the K-1 process where you start with the petition. If they're taking longer to process those petitions than it would take to go through the consular processing, then it doesn't make any sense to do it because it's just adding an extra step to your situation. If they're processing the K-3 visas very quickly recently, then going for the K-3 instead of consular processing will allow you to be together more quickly in the United States. Obviously, that's a wonderful thing for spouses not to have to be separated for too long. That's really going to depend on just current processing times. Another good reason to talk with someone who's been doing that a lot lately.

There is also an option to bring children in that situation. It's called a K-4 visa, very similar to the K-2 except for their parent is already married.

The other option is consular processing, which is the other option for a foreign spouse who is abroad and wants to come into the United States but is already married. Instead of coming on a temporary visa, they actually do the whole process outside of the US so that your spouse would just come into the United States already being a permanent resident, or as it's called colloquially, a "green card" holder. The benefits of that would be it's fewer steps, even though it's still never fast or direct or fun, honestly. However, it's more direct, and people like that. You're done with the process by the time you actually enter the United States.

Another benefit of this process is that the spouse can work immediately when they come into the United States instead of waiting to go through another process, because they're already residents. They don't need any work authorization or anything like that that you would need when you come in on the fiancé visa.

The process for the consular processing case starts with a petition. It's a different type of petition than for the fiancé visas, but it has a lot of similarities. Basically you have to prove that your relationship is a real relationship. You've all heard stories about people trying to pretend that they were married so that they could sneak by immigration. You see that a lot in the movies, although honestly what happens in the movies is usually nothing like the actual immigration process. To prevent that sort of thing from happening, in the petition phase process you have to prove that you have this real relationship and you really have intended to join your lives together. It's not just a trick, a sham, to be able to get a green card.

The petition process is the start. Hopefully you're able to prove that you're legally married, that you love each other, this is the real deal, and they approve that petition. That approval goes again to an intermediate office. It's called the National Visa Center. At that step they ask you for the same information just in a different order on different forms. It's kind of frustrating, but that's just the way the process is. I think they invented that way before they invented computers. It just hasn't been streamlined. That's one of those things I really hope to see at some point in the future. We could get a more streamlined system. For now, this is kind of what we're working with.

Once the petition's approved it goes to the National Visa Center. Once the National Visa Center accepts what you've sent to them, which also one of the main things that the National Visa Center asks for has to do with proof that the American has enough income to support the foreign spouse. That can get a little bit complicated. Sometimes you have to present a lot of financial information. Sometimes even get a second person to vouch for the immigrant and say, "I'll pay for them if they're destitute in the street" or something like that.

Fortunately, I've never actually seen anyone have to fall on that. But getting through that part of the paperwork can be tough. I should mention, I didn't mention the sponsorship documentation on any of the other cases that we discussed. That's an element that's going to come up in a different phase of all of these different types of cases. You're always going to have to prove that if you're going to get a green card through a marriage, at some phase. Fortunately, you can get a joint sponsor if you think you're going to have trouble with that.

We're at the point we're talking about the process for consular processing. Petition, same with the National Visa Center, then it actually is the point where it goes to the embassy, the consulate itself. The process there finishes up with an interview and hopefully you're approved at that point. They give you a visa, but it's actually an immigrant visa which means you're already a resident. They don't actually hand you the card right there, though. You have to come into the United States and they'll mail the card to your house.

At the point where they put that in your passport, the only thing you have to do is come into the United States to finish the process; then you're done. We were talking about how direct the consular processing is. That's why people like it. Just get it done. For some people that's really the only option that they have because they're already married, they're abroad. Maybe if the K-3 visas are taking too long to process, consular processing is what they're going to have to do whether they really like it or not.

One thing I wanted to mention is that sometimes you will see situations where people will try to come into the United States on a tourist visa or, usually it's a tourist visa, but it could theoretically be done with some other type of visa, to avoid doing the consular processing situation. To avoid that whole process, and instead do the process here in the United States. Lawyers vary on their advice as far as that possibility. I do not recommend it mostly because it's actually considered visa fraud.

You never want to do anything that is not completely honest with the US immigration system because it can have pretty big penalties. I just think you should always be as well behaved as possible with immigration and try to get what you need, and keep your ducks in a row and do things that way.

Sometimes people will push it a little bit. It can really border on unethical. The reason people will do it, as we'll discuss, is most people find the process inside the United States, called adjustment of status, to be a little bit more beneficial than some of the other processes. You might be tempted to get around it and try to go for adjustment of status even when you don't really qualify, but I really wouldn't recommend that for those reasons.

For people who maybe have already entered on a tourist visa and they're already in the United States, that's something you really want to discuss with immigration attorney as far as whether you should continue the process in the United States or whether, in your case, it would be best to leave and file from abroad. In most cases you should continue in the US, but that's really going to be a situation that's really going to depend on your personal factors in your case.

That does take us on to the third situation that we see, which is you're either engaged or you're married and your foreign fiancé is currently inside the United States. That's called "adjustment of status." The process to do this inside of the United States. The reason people love this process is that it can be done in one single step, which is really awesome for immigration law because talking about some of the other processes that we mentioned, it's like you go through 3 different offices. Each one's asking for different things. It's kind of a headache and it can take a long time. With adjustment of status you can file a big old, it's a huge pile of documents at one time. You can file it what's called concurrently. You can do multiple types of applications right at the same time. Basically you're filing a petition. You're filing the sponsorship documents. You're filing for the green card. You're filing maybe a few other things at the same time, and it's all at the same time.

Depending on the office that it's being filed at, for example, usually the major cities in the US have a USCIS office they're called. They can process that in a short time. Some areas they're as short as 4 months. That's definitely something that varies by office. There's a way to check that up online at uscis.gov if you're curious what the adjustment of status time frame looks like in your area at any given moment.

One other great thing about adjustment of status is that while the adjustment case is in process, they're waiting for it to process, you can also apply for work authorization. When you send that big packet in at the beginning, you're also, in most cases, almost all cases, I would recommend filing also for work authorization. If they don't process your case fast enough and you've already spent 3 months waiting, you'll actually get temporary work authorization while you're waiting for them to finish processing so that you can actually become a resident.

That's a great thing. You're only waiting a set amount of time to be able to legally work, which is obviously a huge deal for people. They're going to want to be able to work as soon as possible legally.

The process for adjustment of status, you file everything at the same time. They send you a receipt. They send you an appointment to go get your fingerprints and your photo taken. That's called a biometrics appointment. That would happen in your local USCIS office. That's just so they can run a background check on you and make sure that everything you said is true and you don't have some criminal history or terrorist ties that they would want to know about. They call you in for an interview typically, with you and your spouse.

We're actually going to talk a lot about the marriage interview in one of the classes in this series because that's just such a great topic because of all of the rumors and urban legends. It's amazing. Most of them aren't really true, unfortunately, but you do go through an interview, the classic marriage interview, if you're going to do adjustment of status, in most cases. It is legally possible for them to approve you without doing an interview, but at least in my experience, they pretty much require an interview, at least in my particular area where I represent clients most.

The limitations on adjustment of status, there are several limitations which is one reason why everybody's trying to do adjustment of status, but some people just can't. Typically, you have to be here in the United States legally or in some cases, as long as you came in legally and stayed too long, if it's through a marriage you can sometimes adjust your status. For almost all people who came in undocumented, so they didn't come in with a tourist visa, they didn't come in with a student visa, they just walked over or something like that, most people are not going to be able to, who came in that way, are not going to be able to adjust their status and they're going to have to do a different type of process that actually involves going back to a foreign country and going to a consulate and doing lots of other things.

You certainly want to be extremely sure that you know what you're doing before you leave the United States on a process like that because people, unfortunately I've seen cases where people were stuck outside of the United States because they thought they'd be able to get back in and win their case. They legally weren't able to do that. That's just a huge caveat as far as leaving the United States if you're already here.

Some people can't adjust their status, but we're always looking for an advantage to be able to adjust people's status because it's just so beneficial in so many ways. There are a few unusual exceptions where people actually came undocumented and they can adjust their status. For example, there are some people who have a very old family petition back from the year 2000 or something. Some sibling submitted a sibling petition for them or maybe for their parents. There are ways to use these old laws that don't exist anymore. It gets really crazy and really fun for immigration lawyers. That's not a very common situation.

There are also some people who meet an exception where they, for example, might have a child or spouse in the military. There's a special program for them. There are some kind of unusual exceptions. That's why I don't want to say for sure, "If you came in without documents, you can't adjust your status." You definitely would want to find out from an immigration lawyer whether you would qualify or not. Chances are that you probably won't be able to adjust your status if you came in undocumented. That doesn't mean that there's not a way for you to win your case. It's just that that might not be the route that you can use to do it.

There are a couple of other limitations on adjustment of status. There are a couple of types of visas that you can come in on and not be able to adjust your status, which is kind of weird. People will think maybe they'll look online and it will say as long as you came in legally to the United States and you're marrying a US citizen you can adjust your status. That's true in a lot of cases, but it's definitely not true in all cases.

For example, if you came on a fiancé visa, a K-1 like we discussed earlier, with a different US citizen and then you try to adjust after marrying somebody else, it won't let you do that. I've actually seen that happen, that someone tried that and then came to me when it was denied. It's probably not that common that somebody would come as a fiancé and end up breaking up, then the fiancé doesn't leave the country and then eventually marries another American. They're not actually going to be allowed to adjust their status with that second American. That's kind of a weird situation, but that specifically says that in the law.

There are also some people, for example, who come on a J-1 visa, which is some types of exchange students will come on that type of visa. Sometimes they have a 2-year restriction where they actually have to, part of the agreement they've made to come on that particular program is that they're going to leave the United States for 2 years before coming back in. A marriage does not trump that requirement. There might be waivers available, but that's another situation where if you have come in on a J-1 there're going to be some extra steps in making sure that they can really adjust their status or not or figuring out what waiver could be used or if one could be obtained to overcome that problem.

As I mentioned, if you come on a tourist visa intending to get married and adjust your status, that is really not allowed. The way that they figure out … They kind of, USCIS has to look at the circumstances to try to figure out whether they think you are lying or not. They can use things like notes taken by customs officers at the border. If they asked you, "Do you have a girlfriend?" and you said "no," and then you married somebody 2 weeks later. They're going to know that you were lying.

Usually what they look at most is the timeframe of how soon you got married after you came in. If you came in, got married a week later in this huge ceremony and you had a beautiful dress and everybody was wearing matching outfits, they know that you were planning it ahead of time. It's not illegal or fraudulent to, some people came to visit really just to visit. When they were here they realized, "Why have we kept ourselves apart for so long? We're just going to do this. I'm just going to stay in the United States and we're going to live happily ever after." That happens, right? In that case it's okay. Depending on the timeframe and assuming you have cleared this with a lawyer and you've gotten all the factors looked at, in a lot of cases we will go ahead and file an adjustment of status for someone who's come on a tourist visa in that way and decided to stay.

After doing those details about adjustment of status you can see why pretty much everyone who qualifies for an adjustment of status will choose that option. There are a few types of people I've seen who do not choose adjustment of status. They're usually people, for example, who the foreigner needs to travel abroad in the next 3 or 4 months so they don't want to be in the United States the amount of time they would need to let the adjustment process.

I wanted to mention that for some people who are getting an adjustment of status it is appropriate and possible for them to get a travel document, a travel permission, ahead of time in case they need to travel abroad while the adjustment of status is still pending and processing in the office. The problem is just like with the work authorization that you can file, it's probably going to take you 3 or 4 months to get that travel permission. That's why I say that if you know you have to travel abroad or there's a very good chance you're going to have to travel abroad in the 3 to 4 months after you would have filed the case, then that's probably not the best option for you. If you leave without travel permission while your adjustment of status is still pending and hasn't been approved, you're abandoning that case. It doesn't necessarily mean that you can't do something else, you usually can, it's just that you are abandoning this whole case. You've already paid lots of money to the government and probably money to get it prepared by your lawyer. That's why planning ahead is so important.

The other situation where people would not choose adjustment of status are a couple who definitely want to do their legal marriage abroad. They say, "We're in the United States and we're engaged, but we have to do the legal marriage abroad for our personal reasons or religious reasons," or whatever they would like to do. We'll look at consular processing or a K-3 in those cases.

To wrap up then, at least the 3 main situations that we see, we've got the people if your fiancé is abroad and you are in the US and you want to get married in the US, that's a fiancé visa.

If you are already married and your foreign spouse is abroad, and the American could either be abroad or in the United States, and you want to live together in the United States, then that would either be a K-3 visa or consular processing. If you're both in the United States and you meet all the requirements, then that would be an adjustment of status.

Like I mentioned, there are some other options that are a lot more complicated. Some of you may have heard the story about my husband's case, which was so crazy. It was actually the reason that I later became an immigration lawyer, and I honestly love to help people who have totally crazy cases that they think can never be won. It's a beautiful thing if you can win them.

His case was very messed up because he had gotten some really bad legal advice, unfortunately. Our lawyer actually had to use a really unusual process called Humanitarian Parole to get him into the United States because I was here with a family emergency. Then we did an adjustment of status with waivers. Those sorts of cases are very unusual. There are other possibilities that exist, but the ones we talked about today were definitely the most common for the vast majority of couples.

Now that we've covered the basic marriage and fiancé options, I wanted to see if we've got any questions. Megan could you go ahead and explain to the callers how they can raise their hands and how the question and answer session will work?

Megan: Yeah definitely. I see we have a lot of callers on the line here. If you want to ask a question, the question and answer session's been opened. All you have to do is press *6 on your phone now and that will get you into the queue so you can ask your question. I'll then say the last 4 digits of your phone number so you will know it's your turn. I will go ahead and unmute your line and then you can go forward with your question. We'll go ahead now. Anybody who has questions please go ahead and press *6 on your phone.

I think we have quite a few callers here. I'll give you a few more seconds to press *6 if you have a question. Okay, I understand completely that a lot of your questions might be private in nature. You would probably prefer to contact our law office directly and ask to speak with Clare or another attorney at our office. As I'm speaking feel free to go ahead and press *6 if you do have a question.

Our number here is 317-247-5040. Please don't hesitate to call us and we'll put you in touch or get an appointment scheduled so you can meet with Clare or another attorney here.

Again, I just wanted to let you know all of these calls will be recorded. If you have to miss any of them in the future or want to re-listen to one tonight after our last seminar, we will send you all of the links to all 5 seminars shortly after that date and then you can listen to them again.

Also be sure to if you're able to call in tomorrow evening we'll have another seminar at 7:00. Clare will be talking about potential pitfalls you can run into in your case. This is definitely going to be a really important topic to follow up on everything we've learned from tonight. The login info is going to be the same that you used this evening. Feel free to invite your friends to join the call tomorrow in our upcoming seminars. We just recommend that they sign in with us or sign up with us, rather. Have them call us or email us and we can send them the recordings and materials directly like we did for you.

Thank you again everybody for calling in this evening. Thank you for your time. We hope this seminar was helpful and take care. We'll see you back or hear from you tomorrow. Goodnight.

Part 2 – Potential Pitfalls, aka "Grounds of Inadmissibility"

Megan: I think we're going to go ahead and get started this evening. It looks like we have a lot of callers on the line. Good evening, everyone, and welcome to our second call in this series. I'm Megan, and I'll be hosting tonight's call with immigration attorney Clare Corado. Our topic tonight is "Potential Pitfalls in Immigration Cases, also known as Grounds of Inadmissibility." I see that a lot of people from last night's class have joined us again tonight. We're excited to have you all back. I hope you found your first class helpful.

Briefly, for those of you who weren't on the first call, Clare is the founder of the law firm Corado Immigration Law, which is dedicated to helping Americans get citizenship for their foreign spouses.

We will again be recording tonight's call, and we'll be sending recordings from all 5 classes to you a few days after our last class. Just like in our call from last night, Clare will be staying on for a question-and-answer session at the end, so just grab a pen and paper, and jot down your questions as we go along. I will explain later how the Q and A session will work.

Also, if your call gets disconnected, no worries. Just use the same phone number to call back and the same access code, and you'll get right back into the conference call. Let's go to Clare.

Clare, are you ready to get started, then?

Clare: I am. Thanks, Megan. I'm so glad to be on here tonight with everyone. What we talked about last night was the general options that people have if they're looking at a marriage immigration case. So they're either engaged or married to a US citizen or resident, and they're thinking about how they're going to go about the green card process. After we've talked about those basics, tonight we're going to look at some of the types of problems that can actually come up in a case. Those are called "Grounds of Inadmissibility" under immigration law.

I want to talk generally about how immigration law works, to let you guys know the context of what we're looking at here. In immigration law, there are hundreds of different options: visas and ways to get a green card, and other things that aren't visas or residence. They all have different types of requirements. They all have different things that can cause problems; different things that are required to actually qualify; and different benefits that you get if you're able to qualify for the particular program.

Some of the options might allow you to live permanently in the United States, such as getting a green card. Some of them may just allow you to study, or just to go on vacation, or just to ... There are a few different things. Mostly studying and going on vacation are the main ones that we would see. Some of them allow you to live and work temporarily; things like that.

The marriage immigration cases are one subset of types of cases. They are called Family Petitions. We're looking at that particular area. The way that Family Petitions work, and specifically the different marriage cases that we discussed, is the very first stage is, we're going to look and see if the person meets all of the different requirements of the particular program, if the truly have the family relationship. That's what we discussed last night.

Now we're going to talk about the impediments that can prevent you from being able to carry on. In the next call, not tonight but the next call next week, we're going to be talking about if you have any of these problems or Grounds of Inadmissibility, is there a way for you to overcome that problem? We use waivers and other types of exceptions that may apply to overcome some of those problems.

Tonight we're just going to talk about problems. Many of you already know that you have a fiancé or a spouse who meets the initial qualification issue, based on your relationship: that you're married or engaged and you meet the other requirements.

"Grounds of Inadmissibility" sounds like a big mouthful. It's just a legal term for the different problems that can come up once you get past the phase of showing your relationship and you're to the point where the government is checking your background and looking into your history to see whether you're going to qualify or not.

There are tons of different Grounds of Inadmissibility, and tonight we're just going to talk about some of the more interesting ones, and the more common ones. I would not want you to take this call to be the definitive answer on whether the person was admissible or not, or whether they had any Grounds of Inadmissibility. It's very important, as we discussed last night, to make sure you have an expert opinion on that, with an immigration lawyer, before you would ever move forward on your case.

A lot of people are curious about this, you have questions, and so we're going to just talk about the basics. It's interesting: if you look at the Grounds of Inadmissibility, you can really see the history of the United States in the Grounds of Inadmissibility. They have added a lot of things over time, and they don't usually take things away, so we'll see things like ... Being a communist is on the list, or being a part of Nazi Germany is on the list. There are what they call "Moral Grounds of Inadmissibility," that include being a polygamist. Things like that, you can guess when they were all added into the Grounds of Inadmissibility over time, in the history of the US and when we were concerned about particular types of activities and things that popular culture wanted to keep out of the United States.

As far as the Moral Grounds, there are other Moral Grounds of Inadmissibility, aside from polygamy, including prostitution and illegal gambling and things like that. They even have on there ... They say "a habitual drunkard." It's kind of funny, because it's not language you would use anymore, but that's the technical term that they added a long time ago, that people used to call it.

I did want to quickly cover polygamy. People tend to think, "Polygamy definitely doesn't apply to me." I actually do see that come up in some modern cases. The cases I've seen really have to do with cases where someone is an accidental polygamist. A lot of times people will get married abroad, or they'll get married in their home country, and then they'll come to the United States and they don't realize that that marriage in their home country is still considered a marriage in the US. Sometimes people will, before getting a divorce or annulment of their initial marriage abroad, they will get married in the United States again. Technically, that makes them a polygamist.

So that can become an issue, and you definitely want to make sure that if you've ever had anything that could have remotely resembled a wedding in a foreign country, that legally has been dissolved, or at least has been analyzed to make sure that it wasn't a real marriage or a legally binding one. It's kind of interesting. You wouldn't expect that one to come up in modern practice, but I do see it occasionally. Hopefully all of you will have taken care of that issue so that I won't have to help you with that in particular, but if that's already happened I would be happy to help you try to sort that out.

Another one that we see is what are called the "Health Grounds of Inadmissibility." There are some types of contagious diseases that can cause you to be inadmissible. There used to be quite a few things on the list, but fortunately with modern medicine, a lot of chronic diseases, even things as serious as HIV, can be controlled and not prevent a person from coming into the United States. The way that we do see the Health Grounds of Inadmissibility affect cases now is that people have to take a medical exam and pass it before they can actually become residents of the United States.

During that exam, they test for immunity to different types of diseases, and if you don't have it, you have to get a vaccine. There is a list of required vaccines. If you have anything contagious, like potentially active tuberculosis or things like that, you would have to get treatment for that, take the antibiotics, for example, with tuberculosis, and make sure you have a clear chest X-ray. They just want to make sure that people aren't going to come into the United States and get a bunch of people sick. We do see a lot of people needing that treatment, especially if they're from a developing country where things like tuberculosis are common. A lot of times they might trigger the screening test even if they don't actually have it. That's where we get stuck with the Health Grounds of Inadmissibility.

Some people might have a ... When we talk about vaccines, they may have some kind of reaction previously with a vaccine and they are medically unable to get more vaccines. Or, some people may, for moral reasons or there are religious reasons, they may be opposed to receiving vaccines. The US government doesn't look too kindly upon that, but there are some limited exceptions for people who are unable or unwilling to receive the vaccines.

If you wanted to apply for one of those waivers, and we can talk more about waivers tomorrow night but I just want to mention that if you have a lifelong religious objection to certain types of medical interventions and that can be proven, that can be a way for you to get around that. Generally, it's much, much easier to get the vaccines than get around those Health Grounds of Inadmissibility, rather than messing with that. But if it's really important to you, you may be able to make a stand in that way and not be required to do that.

Those are some of the kind of fun and interesting ones that we see. The most common Grounds of Inadmissibility that I see have to do with different types of immigration violations and different problems of people's criminal history. I want to talk about both of those two categories in greater detail. Again, not really specific legal advice, and a lot of these grounds are pretty technically complicated, but we can talk about generally what the grounds are in those two categories.

Probably the most common ones I see these days for immigration violations have to do with time being undocumented in the United States. There is a penalty, or Ground of Inadmissibility, once someone has spent 6 months or more undocumented in the United States, and then there's a different penalty for when they have spent a year undocumented in the United States, or more.

The different Grounds of Inadmissibility have different types of penalties associated with them. For the 6 months' time undocumented in the United States, there is a 3-year penalty associated with it, where you would not be able to come back in the United States unless you got some sort of waiver. For one year undocumented, it's a 10-year penalty, that you cannot come into the United States unless you receive a waiver. We'll talk about waivers tomorrow. In some cases, you may have been here undocumented and yet that Ground of Inadmissibility may not apply to you, because the interesting thing about the Grounds of Inadmissibility for undocumented presence are that the penalties don't apply until you leave the United States.

Sometimes, we have people who, they come in on a tourist visa, and then they were only supposed to stay 6 months but they stayed 10 years instead, and then they're marrying a US citizen, and that's their only legal problem that they have in their history. They would qualify for Adjustment of Status, as we discussed last night, for doing the case inside the United States. They can actually become a resident inside the United States. Since they can do their interview here and do the process here, they don't have to leave the country.

The crazy, illogical thing about it is, if they don't leave the country technically they don't have that penalty, so they don't even need a waiver. I should have mentioned at the very beginning that immigration law is just not always logical, and sometimes it's downright unjust the way that different penalties are applied to different people depending on their country of origin or ability to get a tourist visa. But that certainly is a very beneficial loophole for a lot of our clients. We're happy it exists and wish it were a little more available to even more people.

Another really common immigration Ground of Inadmissibility that we see is having been deported. There are a lot of people out there who believe that they've been deported, and technically, legally, they may not have been deported. There are different types of procedures that can actually happen at the border. Some people will have crossed into the United States, maybe on foot, and then found by a Customs and Border Protection officer. They will go through some sort of paperwork, and some sort of fingerprinting, and then be taken back over to Mexico, for example.

The interesting thing is, some of those processes aren't actually deportations. They can be different types of legal procedures that don't have the same legal effect. So sometimes we're just asking a lot of questions about exactly what happened, what they said to the person, how long the process took, what year it happened in, because depending on the year they used to be doing a lot of these quick little, "Hey, we got your fingerprints," and just dumping people back on the other side of the border, and it didn't have the same legal effect. Now, they're really being very careful to process everyone as a deportation to make sure these penalties apply to people in the future. So it's really interesting, because a lot of people will say, "I've been deported," and then it will turn out that they have not been.

Another interesting thing about that whole immigration side of the Grounds of Inadmissibility, is that it's possible to get a copy of your record with Immigration, with the different branches of the Department of Homeland Security, through what is called a Freedom of Information Act Request. Sometimes it's just not clear at all what could have happened with this particular person. It's not like legal procedures are very clear to the general public, so people just say, "I don't really know what happened, but something happened," so we are able to order a copy and clarify things that way. That can take a really long time, like 6 months to a year, and depending on the office it can take even longer sometimes. But it's good to know that sometimes there is a way to clarify beyond that and figure out what grounds might apply to you before you start a case, because certainly you wouldn't want to start something that's not going to work or that could draw attention to you and put you at risk if you were completely inadmissible and there was no way for us to overcome it.

Being deported is another one. There is a different and separate penalty for having reentered after you've been deported, or for coming in undocumented and staying for a while, and then leaving and coming back in a second time undocumented. They actually have a really strict penalty for those particular actions. Right now, the penalty is a lifetime bar unless you stay outside of the United States for 10 years, and then your spouse gets a waiver for you. It's extremely strict, which I think is really disappointing and really unfortunate for a lot of couples.

If you think that that ground might apply to you, it's super, super, super important that you talk to an immigration lawyer, and make sure that you have all of your dates as specific as possible: when you came in, when you left, because those particular penalties were invented in the '90s, and they took effect at certain dates at that time. So certain people, depending on when their travels were, it may or may not apply to them. Or, if they had only been in the United States a short time, then left and come back, it actually might not apply. It's sort of a technical Ground of Inadmissibility, but it always is a huge red flag if someone has been in and out more than once undocumented. You want to look at it very carefully.

I unfortunately have seen some cases where people have gone with attorneys who maybe don't do a lot of immigration law, and they will mistake that particular Ground of Inadmissibility with being here undocumented for more than a year. They won't realize it's different. But the waiver is different for people who have just been more than a year undocumented. They'll see 10 years and 10 years, and not see that the waiver is different or that it's not available as quickly in the cases where people have been in more than once. You can actually get stuck, unfortunately, abroad, before you realize, "Hey, I actually have to wait 10 years to even apply for the waiver in this case," where in other cases you can apply immediately for the waiver instead of having to wait the 10 years. Again, be very sure you do know what applies to you before you start anything.

Another one that we see a lot is Fraud and Misrepresentation. If the immigrant has ever lied to an immigration officer, maybe when they were coming in on a visa, they told them something that totally wasn't true, or maybe they had applied for a tourist visa in their country and on the questions that said, "Do you have any immediate relatives in the United States?" They had said "No," even though they had a spouse there or maybe they had a parent or someone who they asked about, and they had lied about it.

Unfortunately, we see a lot of places abroad where there are people who prepare documents and they tend to just fill them out how they think will get you the visa that you want, and not based on actual reality. That's a very dangerous thing, and it does lead to some of these Fraud and Misrepresentation issues. There are some people who ... what happened may not technically qualify as fraud or misrepresentation. It has to be something that would have changed the outcome; there are certain requirements for how serious it had to have been, and intentional, and things like that. Sometimes, instead of just agreeing to a fraud Ground of Inadmissibility, will argue that technically it doesn't even qualify. Sometimes that can be successful.

Another immigration Ground of Inadmissibility is for smuggling other immigrants in. Sometimes they will even apply that when you have brought a child with you or something like that. That's a pretty serious one as well.

Those are the main immigration ones, related Grounds of Inadmissibility that we see. I want to move on to the Criminal Grounds. This is again just a really brief overview. There are people who are even sort of specialists in what they call "crimmigration," which is the intersection between criminal law and immigration law. I myself would not say that I'm a specialist in that particular area. I do practice in that, and I have lots of clients who have different types of Criminal Grounds, but I do not represent people in criminal court or anything like that. I just deal with the immigration side of things.

There are entire books written about the Criminal Grounds. This is a very quick overview. That's my caveat about that. Any type of drug crime is extremely serious in immigration law; extremely, extremely serious. There are very few drug crimes that you can do and still be allow inside the United States. A lot of the penalties are permanent. If you ever know of an immigrant or are an immigrant and you're charged with a crime like that, it is very, very crucial that you're working with your criminal defense attorney as well as an immigration attorney, because sometimes things that would just be a total slap on the wrist here in the United States ... If someone is a citizen, it would be like, "Well, you have to do community service now because of that, and it's going to be a misdemeanor," and so you would say, "Okay, I won't do that again," and you sign your plea, and that's what you do ... Some of those similar types of things, if an immigrant were to take that deal, they would be automatically deported and they would never be allowed in the United States again.

They take drug crimes extremely seriously. It's definitely something to look into. There is an exception for some minor possession of marijuana in some cases, but certainly, please stay away from drugs if you're an immigrant, because it really can be kryptonite to your case.

Another major category of crimes that we see in the Grounds of Inadmissibility have to do with crimes involving moral turpitude. "Moral turpitude" is another one of those terms where they wrote it a really long time ago and people don't really talk like that anymore. So there's a lot of argument over the years about what "moral turpitude" really means. Of course, it's very hotly debated. What it generally means is doing something dishonest. You know something is wrong, and you do it anyway.

The kind of crimes that usually fall in that category will be things like ... Stealing something is the classic example; things that have to do with fraud or deception, or that you know you're doing something wrong and you do it. There are a lot of ways in those cases to also argue that this particular crime doesn't actually qualify as a Crime Involving Moral Turpitude. It's frequently abbreviated as a CIMT, because it's a huge mouthful to go around saying, "Crime Involving Moral Turpitude, Crime Involving Moral Turpitude." If you see that, it could either say "CIMT" or "CMT," that's what they're referring to.

There are some crimes that are not actually a Ground of Inadmissibility, but they can hurt you if you need a waiver because they are sort of a negative discretionary factor. Sometimes they will say, "Technically your crime doesn't disqualify you, but you might not merit this particular type of discretion, so we're not going to use it in your favor." An example of that might be something like a DUI. I don't want you to think just because someone might have a DUI they can't do their case, but that's an example where sometimes we might have more trouble in your case, depending on the other factors, if you have a crime like that ... Although technically a DUI isn't a Ground of Inadmissibility and doesn't disqualify you from getting a green card through a family petition in most cases.

One thing that I think is important to mention, though, is that, as I mentioned at the beginning, there are so many different programs available under immigration laws, and for some of them a single DUI will completely disqualify you. Certainly, don't try to get any of those, but you want to make sure that for the particular thing you're trying for, that it's not going to be a problem.

An example of a type of case where a DUI is a huge problem and completely disqualifies you is with the DACA Program. I don't know if any of you have heard of the program for some people who came as children in the United States, and they are able to get a temporary work authorization. One conviction for a DUI in almost all cases will disqualify them, unless in some cases they were able to expunge it or something like that. It's not a good thing, but fortunately for the marriage cases it's also not an automatic bar to being able to get the green card. It just might be something we have to work around or show additional favorable factors, if we're asking for a waiver.

Another Criminal Ground of Inadmissibility has to do with when you have crimes that might not be in any of the categories that are listed, but you have multiple crimes that require a certain amount of jail time or have a certain amount of penalties. That in itself can get you into trouble. There is a list of crimes called "Aggravated Felonies" that are all really, really, very bad for your immigration case, as bad as they sound. The strange thing about them, though, is that we think of local courts and federal courts … What we refer to as a felony is something specific in criminal law, but for immigration law it's sometimes something different. Sometimes people will actually say, "This is a misdemeanor, so it's no problem, and I'm going to take this guilty plea," but in immigration law it's considered an Aggravated Felony. We see that with some of the drug possession crimes.

There is actually a list. If you google the Aggravated Felonies, a lot of them are obviously very serious, the sort of things you would expect, like killing someone or stealing things of very high value. There's a big list of things. Certainly, avoid those. If you have those problems, you've got some bigger problems than just immigration problems. You're probably also going to have prison time before you would be deported. I wouldn't expect a lot of people to be in that situation, hopefully.

We covered the different Criminal Grounds, the main ones that we see, and the Immigration Grounds. There are some other random problems that aren't really exactly Grounds of Inadmissibility but they can certainly put a wrench in the process. For example, if someone has come over on a J-1 Visa, for example, as an exchange student, I think we may have mentioned this yesterday, for some people on that particular visa type, there is actually a requirement that they go back to their home country for 2 years. They're not allowed to come back to the United States without a waiver. It's not a punishment; it's simply because with that particular type of program, type of visa, they are entering into an educational program. The idea is that they're going to get skills in the United States, and they're going to take them back to their home country.

It's part of the agreement that they are actually going to go back to their home country and they're not going to stay in the United States. It's sort of a brain drain out of that foreign country. For some couples, that can be a really tough roadblock, because it seems … Logically, a person would say, "Well, that makes sense, but if they fall in love with an American and that person can't go abroad, it's only fair that they get to stay." Well, I totally agree with you, but that's not how the laws are written. You actually have to get a waiver for that two-year restriction.

Another example, not a Ground of Inadmissibility, but a barrier that we could have, would be if someone has come in on a fiancé visa for a former fiancé and then ended up being engaged or married to a different US citizen, if the first relationship didn't work out and they never became a resident through the first relationship. That's another sort of thing we have to work around, and make sure that our particular approach we're taking is not going to be lost because of that situation.

What happens if you have a Ground of Inadmissibility? I hope I haven't scared you all. It's just to give you some idea of the different types of red flags that we can see. So what happens if you have one of these things? Some of the things have certain time frames associated with them. We mentioned you might have a 3-year penalty or a 10-year penalty. Some of them are considered to be permanent, or they'll say that they are permanent. Even when people say, "Oh, you have a permanent bar," or things like that, in reality some of those bars can actually be overcome with different types of immigration options, such as, for example, if you get a crime victim visa, there are different types of waivers available that can forgive things that the spouse waivers are not able to forgive.

Sometimes I'm seeing a couple, and they come in thinking that we're going to be able to do their case through their marriage, and it turns out we can't for whatever reason, but they have been a victim of a certain type of crime and we're actually able to follow that route instead. We'll use everything we can under immigration law to get the same result, but certainly it has almost always beneficial, if you can do a marriage case, to go that route instead. But don't lose all hope. There may be other options as well for you.

I want you to not be too discouraged until you get a complete and detailed analysis, just to make sure if it applies to you or not. There are some of the Grounds that didn't exist before certain years, and there are some special exceptions. Some of them don't apply if you were a minor when they happened, but some of them do. If you're a minor and you have been here undocumented, it doesn't count against you until you turn 18. Until you're 18 1/2, you don't have that 3- or 10-year bar. Unfortunately, the penalty or the Grounds of Inadmissibility for entering the United States undocumented, then leaving and entering again undocumented ... That actually applies to people even if that happened when they were minors, which is so crazy unfair. If somebody was brought over as an infant and then taken over when they were 5 and then they came back in when they were 6, that's really not their fault.

Right now, the government is applying that penalty, which is kind of crazy. We're really lobbying hard for some changes like that. I had the opportunity fortunately to go with the American Immigration Lawyers Association to lobby Congress about making changes like that. I think it's one of the things where we're going to keep pushing and pushing for some really, really needed changes like that, until they finally do it. Be heartened, because we are just going to keep pushing until we get some of those changes, certainly, for some of our clients.

And, as I mentioned, there are lots of different types of waivers available, so even if one of these things applies to you, it's not the end of the story. Maybe we will overcome the problem. So please don't give up hope. One of the most interesting and complicated areas of immigration law is when you start looking at which grounds apply to you and how can that be overcome or if there's a way to do that. It's really ... A lot of immigration lawyers, and definitely me included, enjoy that challenge of trying to help people overcome these problems that they have in their cases. That's definitely an option for you.

Megan, now that we've talked about some of these different difficulties that we see in clients' cases, let's go and see if anybody wants to ask a question, or if they're feeling shy tonight. Can you go ahead and explain how they can raise their hands and get in line?

Megan: Yeah, sure. Definitely. I just initiated the Q and A session. If anybody has a question, just go ahead and press *6 on your phone now. That will get you into our queue, and then you'll be in line to ask your question. I'll just say the last 4 digits of your phone number, so you'll know when your line has been unmuted, and then you can go ahead with your question. Please just be sure to introduce yourself. Use only your first name for privacy's sake since we are recording this.

I see we already have somebody in line for a question. The phone number, last 4 digits, is 7787. I will go ahead and unmute your line. 7787, are you here with us?

Speaker 3: Hi. My name is Gloria. I think you said that some people can get documents by being the victim of a crime. How does that work exactly?

Clare: Thanks, Gloria. That is a great question. Actually the crime victim visas are one of the most common case types that we're doing right now, just because of the status of current law, so I'm glad you asked that question. There's a separate law that gives a visa called a U Visa, to people that have been victims of certain types of crimes. There's a list inside of the law that lists, "This crime and this crime and this crime." The crimes that are on the list typically are things that involve a violence, like domestic violence or being kidnapped or things like that.

Probably the least serious, I don't want to say that but, the least serious thing that we see that still qualifies would be if you're mugged, someone pulls out a gun and robs you, that's something that qualifies. But it's something we'd have to really look at the police report to see if you qualify. Say you've been a victim of the qualifying crime. You then have to cooperate with the police or with the prosecutor, to help them actually bring justice to the situation. Really, the visas were invented to help the police and the prosecutors do their job and get criminals off the street. So you have to answer their questions or identify people, or whatever they request, and kind of help to bring justice and help them to do their job.

If you do that, then we have to ask the police, or the prosecutor, or Child Protective Services, or whichever authority was involved in investigating the case, we have to ask them to sign something proving that you did help them out and that it was the particular type of case. If we can get that signature, which is sometimes the tricky part, then we can apply to Immigration. It's a very long process, with the crime victim visas, and it does take a couple of years at least. It starts out with the work permit, which you can use to get a social security card, which you can use in most states to get a driver's license, things like that. Eventually, after you've had that for 3 years, you can actually apply to become a resident and get a green card like everyone else, and then a citizenship eventually.

That's why it's great for some people who can't get a green card through marriage; they may be able to eventually do it through the U Visa. The U Visa waiver allows them to forgive almost everything. You still have to ask for it, you still have to argue that you deserve it, but that forgiveness is available. That's why I mentioned that particular type of visa. Does that kind of answer your question?

Speaker 3:	Yes, it does. Thank you.
Clare:	Okay. Thank you.
Megan:	Do we have any other questions this evening? Again, all you have to do is press * 6 and that will put you in line, and I can unmute your line so you can go forward with your question. I'll give you a couple seconds just to make sure.
	Okay. Here we have another question. The last 4 digits of the phone number is 3687. 3687, your line has been unmuted. You can go ahead and introduce yourself and go forward with your question.
Speaker 4:	Thank you, Clare, for such a nice session. My name is Sadhya. My question is related to a lie to an immigration officer. I would like to ask you, what if somebody applies for an F-1 Visa, and at the time of the application the person is not married, and he just filled out the application form by saying that he does not have any immediate relative in the US, and then he gets the F-1 Visa and gets married and comes to the United States on the F-1 status. You know what I mean? He gets married after the F-1 Visa but before coming to the US. Still, it will be considered as a lie for application purpose, or for immigration purpose?
Clare:	That's a great question, and I do want to say first of all that, to be entirely sure, I would want to talk with that person and spend a good 20 or 30 minutes going through exactly what happened, but I think I can give you a general idea. What you're saying is, he applied for a student visa and said he wasn't married, and they gave him the student visa, but before he came to the US he got married and then came in with his wife. Is that what you mean?
Speaker 4:	Yeah. Exactly.
Clare:	Okay. One of the things about the lies or the misrepresentations is that they have to change the result of whether they ... It's going to depend a lot on whether his lie

caused them to be more likely to give him the student visa. In a lot of cases, I would think it wouldn't matter, if they would have given him the visa, and his wife, then it might not matter.

Was his marriage in the foreign country, or did he get his student visa and then come in and get married?

Speaker 4: The marriage? Basically he applied for the student visa, but he was not married at that time. His files will be in the United States. He gets the F-1 Visa and then he gets married. So the United States citizen goes back to his country, gets married with him, so he already got the F-1 Visa, and now he is married to the United States citizen in his country. Now he is coming to the US. Does it make any ...

Clare: Sure. Situations like that, it's going to really depend on how the facts are presented and argued, and the government will argue, "He said this, but he wasn't being truthful at the time. We would have made a different decision if he would have told us." They could make that argument. They may choose to. And his lawyer would try to make the argument that at the time, whenever he said whatever he said, it was true. Sometimes people say, "I'm just coming to visit," or, "I'm going to be a student," and then when they get to the US it's like, they change their mind. They meet somebody, they fall in love, or they spend more time with the person they've been dating and they decided, "Hey, we're going to go forward with this." That's allowed.

When we see cases like that, the government likes to follow a rule of thumb where, if you get married or you make some kind of major change in your status in less than a month, less than 30 days after you get to the US, they're going to assume that you were lying, because it's not very likely that you would have said one thing, come to the US, and like 2 weeks later done something different. But after more time has passed, it gets a little bit easier to show that you just changed your mind. It might be a situation that would come down to that. Like I said, that would be a case where I would go into very great detail with that person to figure out exactly what happened, and how likely it was that that affected the officer's decision about giving him that F-1 Visa.

Speaker 4:   All right. Thank you very much.

Clare: Yeah. That was a great question. Thanks.

Megan: Okay. Do we have any other questions? Again, it's just * 6. I'll give you a couple seconds again, just in case somebody has a question. It looks like we do have somebody else. Give me one second and I will unmute your line.

               Okay. It looks like the last 4 digits of the phone number is 7715. 7715, I went ahead and I unmuted your line.

               [Silence]

Clare: Can you hear us? Can you ask your question?

Megan: I think they might have ... 7715, are you still there? Nope. I think that they're not with us. I don't see any other questions in the queue, so we'll go ahead and wrap this session up. I know that some of you, I still see a lot of people on here, might not want to ask your question because it's personal. We completely understand that. Please don't hesitate; feel free to contact our office and set up a consultation so you can speak with Clare or another attorney in the office. They can analyze your personal situation and help you understand what your options are. If you have a pen and paper, our phone number is 317-247-5040.

               I'm sorry, actually we do have a question here in the queue. We will go to that question. Let's try it again. The last 4 digits of this phone number is 9989. 9989, your line is unmuted. Are you there?

Speaker 5:   Yes, I'm here. Hi, this is Karen. I was just wondering if it would still count if the crime was committed a long time ago.

Clare:	Yes, Karen. That's a great question. A lot of times in law there are strict time limits about how you can do things. Statutes of limitations, we call them. Fortunately, with crime victim visas, that's another one of the awesome things that allows us to do those for a lot of people, is that there is really no time limit as far as when the crime happened. We have people who were a victim 5 years ago, or even 10 years ago, and we've still been able to help them with that. It does get harder when more time passes, to still find the police reports or to still get in contact with the police or the prosecutor so they will sign your form. If you have an opportunity, I would say definitely get help with that as soon as you can. But even if it has been a while, it doesn't necessarily mean you can't do it. If you know someone like that, or that's your situation I would say talk to me, talk with me or some other immigration lawyer and see if you can move forward with it. It could be a really great opportunity for you.
Speaker 5:	Okay. Perfect. Thank you so much.
Clare:	Have a good night.
Speaker 5:	You as well.
Megan:	I don't see any other callers in the queue to ask questions. Thank you all so much for your patience with technology. Technology can be great, but sometimes it can be a struggle. Thanks, everybody, for your great questions. Again, for those of you that are on there that are hesitant to ask your question online, our phone number is 317-247-5040. You can set up a consultation to speak with Clare. Like I mentioned earlier, all of the recordings for all five classes will be available after our last class. We'll email all five of those to you.
	Also, our next class will be next Tuesday at 7 p.m. Clare will be doing the counterpart to tonight's call. Today she talked about the potential pitfalls. In the next class she'll be explaining how waivers can overcome some of these obstacles. Basically, it's like the second half of tonight's call.
	The login info will be exactly the same. Feel free to invite

your friends to join the call, but we do recommend that they call us and sign up directly with us so we can get them the recordings and the materials directly. Thank you all so much for being with us tonight. For now, take care, and we'll see you back next call.

Part 3 – Overcoming the Obstacles with Waivers

Megan: Okay, it's 7:00 and good evening everyone. We're going to get started. This is the third call in the series. I'm Megan and I'll be your host for tonight's call with attorney Clare Corado who many of you know is an immigration lawyer and she's devoted her career to working with couples. Our topic for tonight is Overcoming Obstacles with Waivers.

Again, I just want to let you know that we will be recording tonight's call and sending the recordings from all five classes to you a few days after the last class. Without further ado, let's get started.

Clare, can you hear me?

Clare: Yes, thank you Megan. Tonight's topic is waivers, and I'm really excited because this is one of my favorite topics in immigration law. Thank you all for joining us. You know last time we talked about the grounds of inadmissibility, or the different problems that someone can have that can prevent them in some cases from being able to get their green card and their eventual citizenship. Today we're going to talk about the other side of that, which is – if you have a ground of inadmissibility that applies to you, what can you do to overcome the problem?

In many cases we can use different types of waivers to fix the problem so that the person can actually receive a green card despite the problem that they have. That side of things is really my job, trying to overcome these problems that people have, and I really love it. Some of you may have heard the story of how I got into this whole thing, but basically my husband had a really crazy case. He was scammed when he first came into the United States by a non-lawyer and then we got a lot of bad legal advice as we were engaged and married. He had grounds of inadmissibility for being here undocumented and some of the paperwork that had gone wrong.

Eventually a really good lawyer helped us untangle all that craziness and got him the waivers that he needed and through that process I saw how awesome it is when someone can help you overcome these serious problems that you have and just give you the best gift ever, which is the ability to be with your family in the United States and to have your freedom. We just love it when we find people who say "we've been told we can never do anything", or "we talked to lawyers and they say oh my gosh that's a big old mess, I don't even want to look at it," and we are able to help them. That's really what we do around here.

I'm glad that you're on the call and if any of you are in this situation, my firm would love to help you talk about your individual case and see if there's anything we can do. One quick caveat before we get started is that this is just general information about waivers, so when you get to the question of whether a ground of inadmissibility applies to you, and whether there's a waiver to overcome it, that's one of the most complicated parts of immigration law, so please don't use this information to self-diagnose or take this as legal advice for your particular case. Plus, the law changes pretty quickly and so by the time you listen to this there could already be some changes in immigration law. That's kind of the blessing and the curse of immigration law, it's tough to keep up with. That's why it's my full-time job to stay on top of all the changes.

On the other hand, sometimes the law doesn't help you right now, but the good thing is it'll probably change tomorrow, so in some cases it's a waiting game; to wait until you can do what you want to do and just to keep track of those changes.

Really I'm hoping this call can give you an idea of what's out there, kind of how waivers work, and hopefully that information will help you formulate some great questions for when you go into consult with an immigration lawyer about your specific case and get that personalized information that you're looking for.

What I'd like to do tonight is to break down waivers into the most basic and common things that I see in these types of cases. Just like with the grounds inadmissibility, there is a lot going on in this area of law.

But first let me tell you what I'm not going to talk about tonight.

I'm not going to talk about any waivers for any types of cases other than waivers available to happily married couples. There are waivers out there for crime victims, people who are applying for crime victim visas, people who have been abused spouses, people who are federal informants usually in witness protection, people who want a tourist visa, waivers available in certain immigration court cases if you have to go before an immigration judge, waivers for people who came as refugees. There are a bunch of other waiver out there. This call is not going to cover the whole universe of waivers by any means, and we probably won't even cover all of the waivers available to married couples, but just the ones that we see every day and the most common questions that we receive. Talking about those other waivers might be a great topic for another day because some of them are very exciting.

In general, one great thing about being married to a US citizen, or maybe a permanent resident who's hoping to becoming a US citizen soon, is that you really have a lot of advantages under the law that other types of immigrants don't have. Especially as far as waivers. I think the government has recognized that a marriage is a really special relationship and I think US citizens deserve all the advantages they can get to keeping the love of their lives with them and being able to stay in the United States.

They have reflected that policy in the laws. It doesn't go nearly as far as I would like in some situations, but we do have a lot to work with, so that's a great thing. Some of these waivers are not even available to other types of close family relationships. There's a class of immigrants called "immediate relatives" in immigration law that have a lot of advantages, but even in some cases they even another type of immediate relative, like maybe a parent of a US citizen who's 21, they're an immediate relative and they have some advantages but they still don't have all the same waivers available. So yeah! Take a little mini celebration here about the extra waiver opportunities that you're going to have as a married couple.

The most common type of waiver that we see in our office is for undocumented presence. These waivers apply in cases where someone has been in the United States undocumented. What does that mean? For some people it's that they came in without documents, they walked over, or something like that and are here in the United States without any status at all. For other people, maybe they came with some type of status like a tourist visa. They came for a visit, buts they ended up staying and they've been here for years and obviously their valid stay expired a long time ago and they probably have a job here and everything like that, so they're out of status. They've lost that tourist status. We see that a lot with different types of student visas too. Maybe someone, they start school and then some-thing happens. They drop out of school and start working, and before they know it they've been here undocumented for a while.

Those are both examples of people having "unlawful presence," which is what it's called in immigration law. There's sort of a, before we talk about the different waivers for those issues, I want to mention that there's a really strange thing about unlawful presence here in the United States or about the rules of unlawful presence. The strange thing is that the different grounds for inadmissibility for unlawful presence, they aren't triggered, they don't apply, until the immigrant who's unlawfully present actually leaves the United States.

When I tell people that in consultations, they just look at me like that's the dumbest thing I've ever heard. I kind of have to agree; it's completely illogical. If you're here in the United States and you have unlawful presence and there's a way for you to fix your situation in the United States, well you don't even need these waivers because the penalty doesn't even apply to you because you don't have to leave the United States. It's a very catch-22 type situation.

The problem is going to be for people who under the law don't qualify to fix their situation here in the U.S., they don't qualify to do the marriage case through what's called an adjustment of status, and if you missed the first call about the different ways that the cases are done, you can re-listen to that recording once we send them out when we're finished with all the classes, so that you can hear about that and the different ways it's done.

Not everyone can fix their case here in the United States. If they have to leave and do an interview in their home country and they've been here undocumented, that's where the problem comes in. Because basically they're forced to do the interview in their home country and as soon as they leave, in most cases, then they're going to have this penalty for having been here undocumented. That's where the waivers come in for that particular case.

Depending on how long a person has been here undocumented, when they leave, they will either have a three-year or a ten-year bar where they can't come back unless they get the waiver. For a lot of our clients they have the ten-year bar because they've been here a year or more undocumented, and so that's the waiver we get most often.

Another type of waiver, or type of issue that we can get waived is someone having been deported before. Sometime they're here in the United States, maybe they're here only a short time or maybe they've been unlawfully present for a while, they are deported and they are back in their home country. Now a lot of people will refer to the method for getting them back as a waiver. There's a waiver to get them back. Technically in immigration law it's not a waiver, it's applying for "permission to reapply for admission." That's just a big mouthful, but essentially in practice it is a waiver for that particular problem.

Some other types of issues do have waivers available, although the waivers are nearly not as favorable in their terms as the waivers for the three or ten year bars, are for people who have entered the United States undocumented, spent a fair amount of time here, and then left, and then come in undocumented a second time. Also, maybe, people who have been deported and then reentered the US. In some situations, that can be resolved eventually. However, for these particular problems the immigrant has to spend 10 whole years outside the United States before even applying to try for the waiver. So it's a much harsher penalty than the normal 10-year bar for unlawful presence over one year.

The next type of waiver that we do see sometimes is waivers for fraud or misrepresentation. We had discussed that this is a ground of an inadmissibility. This applies to people who have previously lied on an application or to an immigration officer or a customs officer. Whatever their lie or the misrepresentation was actually caused the officer to make a different decision than he or she probably would have made if the person had told the whole truth or represented the truth as it actually is. For example, they may have presented a fake visa. There's a waiver available for people who've done that in some cases. If the fake documents were something claiming to be a U.S. citizen, like a fake birth certificate, that is a much more serious situation and can't be undone except in very limited circumstances.

There are also waivers available for certain types of criminal history. We had discussed this as well, there are a lot of crimes that won't cause a person to be inadmissible. Please don't take that as permission to go get into trouble, but some things directly won't be automatically disqualifying you. One thing I had mentioned, for example, is driving under the influence of alcohol. It's definitely not a good thing and it's dangerous and all those sorts of things, but for the marriage cases, it doesn't automatically disqualify you either. You wouldn't need a waiver for example for almost all different types of DUI cases you wouldn't actually need a waiver for it unless other things were going on at the same time or if it involved drugs or things like that. However, something really important to keep in mind is that any criminal activity at all, including DUIs, can make it harder to get a waiver for another issue like unlawful presence, because the government official has the discretion to decide whether you deserve to get the waiver. Any criminal activity at all is considered a negative factor in that determination. So when we are doing applications in cases like that, we take extra care to present as many positive factors as possible so that the overall balance is in favor of our client.

People sometimes need waivers for things like a "crime involving moral turpitude," which as we had discussed is a previous call, is just a crazy term in immigration law that classifies a lot of crimes such as stealing things or things that are kind of inherently dishonest. So sometimes we have clients who have some minor crimes like that that they do need to get them waived.

Now there are a lot of crimes out there that you can't waive even with the criminal waivers, so it is extremely, extremely important to have that case analyzed very well to make a strategy before you're trying to do that at all, because you definitely wouldn't want to start a case if that's not something that can be ultimately won. And, at the same time, we never would want to admit that a ground of inadmissibility applies to a client unless we were 100% sure that we, the person was definitely subject to that ground of inadmissibility. In some cases, we'll have people who, you know they've had some incident that they've told me about that it might be a fraud or misrepresentation or it's pretty close to that gray area for misrepresentation, or their particular criminal activity from the past is kind of in a gray area, a lot of times we're going to wait and see whether immigration tells them they're inadmissible based on that basis before we're going to admit it and file a waiver application.

We're going to be prepared for it, obviously, but we're not going to accept any more problems than they're arguing. Even in some cases we've seen cases where when people are at the Consulate, for example, at the US Embassy abroad, they're told that they're inadmissible for a certain reason and really, if you do the legal analysis, it's not true that the person's inadmissible for that reason. So sometimes instead of a waiver we're actually just making an argument that we don't even need a waiver because this doesn't shouldn't even apply to this person and you made a mistake. We've had success with that as well, which is always a really good thing when we're able to do that as well. In a lot of those cases at the Consulate, we are hired once the problem has already happened, usually because of how the original case was presented by the client. They may have presented the facts in a way that caused immigration to believe the ground of inadmissibility applied to them even though it didn't. There is an art to presented what needs to be in the applicable without opening the client up to lines of inquiry that cause problems. Obviously, we are always going to be 100% truthful with every answer and all information in the application. However, immigrants sometimes make their cases much more complicated by volunteering unnecessary information or phrasing things in a way that triggers some red flags.

For the criminal history waivers there are a lot of things they unfortunately don't waive. The more serious crimes, even some crimes that you might not think, you know the average American would not think would be particularly serious, they might not waive. For example, a lot of drug charges, even if they're kind of minor crime classified as a misdemeanor, a lot of times don't have a waiver for them. Yeah, drug charges generally are a huge problem, and so if you have anything like that in your history you want to be extra super-duper sure before you do anything relating to the case at all. But there are waivers available for some criminal issues.

We've talked about a few of the different types of waivers that we see most commonly. I wanted to talk a little bit too, another question I get a ton which is "okay, so if there's a waiver available does that mean I automatically get it? Or what do you actually have to do to get a waiver?" We sometimes even get calls in our office where people will say "Hey what do you charge for a waiver" or "Hey can you fill out our form for a waiver? That's the only thing we need you to do." I can tell from that type of question that there's a lot of misunderstanding about who gets a waiver and why and how difficult it is to actually get it.

The waivers are not something where there's just a form available and they just, okay, you qualify for the opportunity to apply for a waiver and so here it is. Of course there are forms involved, but that is such a minor part of the whole application. If you qualify for a waiver it just means in your particular circumstance it is possible that you can get a waiver, but it doesn't mean you're going to win the waiver. And waivers are actually one of the hardest things in immigration law. They take a lot of effort, a lot of legal arguments, and they need to be completely customized to each individual client for the best result. I have seen some cases where a client was given a standard list of evidence to collect for a waiver by a lawyer. If you have that situation, run away fast. There is no standard list of waiver evidence. At our office we have a very in-depth conversation with every couple and create a customized waiver strategy. We have to first formulate the legal arguments, and only then can we go about finding the best evidence to support those arguments.

So let's talk about what kind of legal argument we use in waiver cases and kind of what the standard is that the government's using.

I'm going to just lump together all the different main types of things we have to show for waivers. There are some distinctions between the different types of waivers I've mentioned. When you are trying to get permission to apply for a green card after a deportation, that has a different standard than getting a waiver for your unlawful presence. But I don't think you guys really care about those details. That's more something I would teach in a class to other attorneys, so we're not going to go to that level of detail.

Generally, there are two main things that we look at when we're trying to get a waiver. They are extreme hardship to the US citizen, the spouse, and discretion. Discretion means whether the person deserves to get the waiver, whether they're a good upstanding person. I want to go into a lot more detail about that, but those are the two main things that we're usually dealing with when we are working on a waiver.

"Extreme hardship" is a technical term in immigration law, and when you think extreme hardship a lot of people will say, "Hey I've got extreme hardship. If I can't get this waiver, my husband or wife is going to be in a foreign country for 10 years and our kids are going to be traumatized and our marriage is going to be ruined and who knows what's going to happen to them if they're in a country that's unstable. They could even be killed by rampant gang violence." And I personally completely agree that this would be really terrible and I personally think that it should count as extreme hardship. I mean come on, that's totally extreme hardship and it's an awful, awful thing for a family to have to face.

Unfortunately, under the legal definition of extreme hardship those things don't really matter at all for your waiver. In fact, submitting a waiver that proved all of those things would actually be the worst waiver attempt ever. The legal standard for what qualifies as extreme hardship is that your hardship goes above and beyond what would happen to any family, to any marriage where one of the spouses was deported and separated. The government would say the fact that your marriage is going to break up and your kids are going to have this trauma and your life is going to be totally off track because you're separated and all these things are going to happen, they would say that's pretty much what we expect when a someone's deported or can't fix their immigration situation. There's nothing special about that situation, and sadly enough, the U.S. government actually does deport people like that every day.

Every year there are hundreds of thousands of people, unfortunately, families that are separated which is heartbreaking to me. Through our work we try to do everything we can to reduce the number of families that are going to actually face that. It is a really tragic, inhumane thing that is happening right now in this country. I have lobbied legislators in Congress for immigration reform on behalf of the American Immigration Lawyers Association. I try show the legislators what is actually going on as a result of these policies. I try to put a face on it, show the real people who are devastated by these policies every day. I think is so incredibly important. Plus, they realize that us immigration reform advocates are going to keep showing up, and showing up, and pushing, and pushing, until we get the changes we need.

So back to the legal standard for waivers. So the government doesn't really care about those basic core hardships. They're looking for extreme hardship. That means that the family would suffer, or specifically the US citizen spouse would suffer a hardship that's above the normal hardship that would come from being separated from a spouse for 10 years.

Sometimes I think if we don't explain that well enough to our clients they're a little bit offended because we're looking for these special details and they're saying, "Look we're going to be separated for 10 years, isn't that extreme hardship enough?!" We have to just explain that unfortunately we're playing this legal game, which it's sad to call it a game because it's people's lives at stake, but there's a certain way the waivers are done, and it's not what a logical person would think that they would care about that they actually do care about. But we need to work within the current legal system to have the best chance of winning the waiver.

When we're trying to figure out what people's extreme hardships are, we sit down for a nice long meeting with our clients and we go through lots and lots of details of their lives and try to figure out different things that we could possibly use for an extreme hardship argument. It's going to be a very personal argument for each particular client.

Here are some of the classic categories that we go through to try to figure out if there are some good classic arguments in there for extreme hardship and then of course there are going to be some other individual factors that would be entirely personal to the couple. Usually I like to start by asking people if there are any medical conditions, any health problems in anyone in the family. We like to get as much detail as possible about anything that may have happened. The most important type of medical conditions are ones that are actually suffered by the US citizen, but sometimes we can use arguments that the, you know, if the children are suffering from some type of medical condition that it actually is a hardship to the US spouse because to watch their children suffer, or to have to take their children abroad where they can't get medical treatment, that would be an extreme hardship.

In some cases, if the immigrant has a very serious medical condition we can actually even use that argument. Just to be clear, the government doesn't care if the immigrant would suffer extreme hardship, at least for these particular types of waivers, but they do care if the immigrant's suffering and the citizen spouse's knowledge of that suffering would cause the citizen themselves to suffer extreme hardship. I don't know if that makes sense but basically, we can pretty much present the information in a way that always shows that it's the US citizen who is having the extreme hardship, which is what the argument we have to actually make.

First we check for any kind of medical conditions. We want to know about everything. People usually start by saying, "I don't have any medical conditions." We'll say, "Really? You've never had a surgery, you've never been to the hospital, you've never gone to the doctor for anything?" And a few things will come out. And so a lot of times even things that people might not think of as being an extreme hardship can be legally turned into an extreme hardship depending on how they are presented. We will get the medical records, and we can look at possible future complications of those medical conditions, or the possibility of passing them onto their children, or what would happen if they were in a foreign country when there was a relapse or a trigger or something like that. We'll look at whether not having the medical care is available in the foreign spouse's country.

There are a lot of ways that we can use those medical conditions to actually make an extreme hardship argument. I do want to mention that we would never lie on a waiver application. Obviously, I'm a lawyer I would never tell a lie to the government, I would never represent someone that I knew was lying or anything like that. But for waiver cases it's all about how you present the information. We're going to look for things that are true and we're going to present them in a way that shows that it could cause extreme hardship to the person. We're going to say, "What is the worst-case scenario for this couple?" And we're going to present all of the evidence that this worst-case scenario could feasibly happen.

Another area that we look at is financial hardships. There is a certain amount of hardship that would be expected of anyone who was separated for 10 years or the spouse went back to their country where their earnings were lower, so we're looking for something above and beyond that. Sometimes if the US citizen has gone to school and they have significant student loan debt or they have some kind of medical debt, or they have a lot of financial responsibilities here in the United States that they can't, they're not going to be able to pay off if they leave, then sometimes part of the argument will have those financial elements of it too.

Sometimes if the foreign spouse had to be in their home country for 10 years, the US citizen spouse and the children would not be able to survive here financially based on their particular situation. That can sometimes be a way to make a financial argument as well.

We also make arguments about the US citizen spouse's education or their credentials or their career. A lot of our US citizen spouses have gotten some type of degree or they have some type of license, for example they might be a nurse or a teacher or something that requires some type of professional license or certification, some type of training or exam. So a lot of times if they were to go, say we have someone who's a nurse, well if they were to follow their spouse into the foreign country then they couldn't just pick up being a nurse in a foreign country even if they did speak the language because that country has its own rules about nursing and they would have get an education all over again, or take exams or something like that. So they would completely lose that part of their, what do I want to say, not their personality, but that part of their life and it's not something they could recover from very easily. Sometimes their professional side of things comes into play with those arguments.

We also look at their children. Sometimes we have clients who maybe have children from a prior relationship or a prior marriage and in almost all of those cases those kids have custody orders, so our US citizen clients actually couldn't just pick up their kids and take them to a foreign country. They wouldn't be allowed to by the courts. Sometimes we can show extreme hardship in that they would either have to choose between their spouse or their children because they basically can't just abandon their other children here and they're not allowed to take them with them. The children would then lose the relationship with their other parent, so it just would be an extreme hardship for the US citizen. That's a frequent argument as well.

There are some arguments that can be made related to some language and cultural issues for the US citizen spouse, you know if they don't speak the language that's spoken in the foreign country and for some reason it would be difficult for them to pick it up, that can be an argument. That's a pretty common argument so I usually use that one as a piggy-back on other types of arguments.

As far as cultural, usually the times when we'd use a cultural argument would be things like, say the spouse is from Saudi Arabia, or someplace where, and it's an American woman, and the American woman, for an American woman it would be an extreme hardship to have to go somewhere where women can't drive, they have to stay covered from head to toe, and they need a male supervision at all times. It's just that is not something that we can stand, honestly, as American women and we shouldn't have to. So in some cases that would be an extreme example, but there are other countries that maybe have some level of argument that could be made that because of the extreme cultural differences it would be a hardship for the American citizen.

When we're talking with people we go through a lot of these different possibilities. Another one that we talk with them a lot is about any past trauma that the person has had. Any past counseling or mental health issues they may have had. A lot of times when people have been through stressful times in their life they could be okay now and we hope that they are, but undergoing another extreme stressor of having to either move abroad or lose your spouse, can really be a significant factor for that sort of thing. Sometimes there are arguments there.

Another one is if our clients have ever suffered some type of loss in their life. Maybe their father left the family at an early age, or someone passed away who they were very close to, or some relationship broke up unexpectedly, they can be especially emotionally vulnerable because of that prior incident. That can be an argument that they have hardship that's more extreme than what other people might have if this is their first situation like that.

I know that sounds completely terrible that we, that the government would consider the current loss to be not as terrible if it were the first time, but as much as I dislike that part of the system I do use the system to my clients' advantage, and that's kind of what we have to do in these cases.

One thing that I did want to mention about extreme hardships is that historically there have been two ways that we have to show extreme hardship. We have to show that the American citizen would face extreme hardship both if they were separated from their spouse for the period of time, 3 or 10 years, or if they had to move themselves and their family to the spouse's foreign country to be with them. So we would have to show that neither of those options were viable because both of them would lead to extreme hardship.

There are currently sort of an interesting, like I said there are always changes in immigration law, so right now they're undergoing an interesting process where the government, USGIS specifically, is going to try to give us some more specific guidelines about exactly what the best arguments are for extreme hardships, what should count, what's not as good of an argument. Because up until now it's been a little bit of a free for all. Other than knowing that it has to be hardship above and beyond the normal hardship that would be suffered by the family if they were separated, we don't have a lot of guidance other than experience and seeing what works and trying things out. It's that accumulated experience over time.

I'm hoping, although it has not been finalized at this time, that we get more concrete guidance. There was some draft guidance released, so some ideas of what the guidance might look like and we were allowed to comment on that. They are taking those comments into consideration. If they do come up with a final document and it looks like the draft document that we saw, they're actually talking about not requiring us to show extreme hardship in both situations.

Right now if you can only show that yes, there's extreme hardship if they're separated but we can't show extreme hardship if the whole family goes over to this foreign country, well then we can't get the waiver. Or if the opposite is true, theoretically you also couldn't get the waiver. I have to say that's never actually happened to us, that we've proved one and not the other. It's just something that we have to present when we're doing the actual waiver application.

However, the idea that's being floated is maybe not requiring applicants to show both. If you could show extreme hardship either way with just one of them, then that might be enough. That's going to be a really interesting development in waiver practice and waiver law to see where that goes.

Those sorts of guidance and just experiencing what's working and what's not, is really important to us when we're formulating our cases because we are constantly trying to give everyone the best advantage and see what's working. That's going to be something to kind of keep an eye out for as far as whether that's going to change or not.

That's what I wanted to say about extreme hardship. As far as the other side of what we have to show in some waiver cases, and it's always a good idea to show at least a little bit in all waiver cases I would say, is the discretionary side of things.

The discretion means whether this person deserves to get a waiver, whether in looking at their history does the official who's making the decision think, "Hey, this is a good person, and I think they'll make a good resident of the United States," or have they been in all other sorts of trouble and they just seem, I don't know, kind of sketchy. The deciding official kind of makes a personal decision based on their own, I don't want to say totally on their own experience or their own ideas, but it's a judgement call they have to make looking at the positive and the negative factors of the case to decide whether it should be granted or not.

Discretion is kind of tough. I mean, extreme hardship is tough too, but when you look at a discretionary argument like that, sometimes things that don't technically disqualify the person like I'd mentioned earlier with the DUIs or the driving under the influence charges, you know it doesn't automatically disqualify someone from winning their green card through marriage, but it can be really negative in a discretionary, from a discretionary standpoint. Maybe the person has great extreme hardship and they qualify otherwise but they have three DUIs. It's going to be a lot harder for us to also convince the officer that the person really should receive the waiver and that they deserve it.

In cases like that we really work very hard to show that the person has rehabilitated their lives that there are lots of other good contributions to society that they're making and really dig around into that side of thing. But they basically say that it's a, what they call a balancing of equities. They're going to look at the positives, they're going to look at the negatives and decide whether you deserve it. If you deserve it they say that they will exercise favorable discretion is the term that they use. We always have to go after that too.

There are a couple of sort of rumors, well there are more than a couple of rumors out there about waivers, but a couple things I wanted to mention that I hear and see floated around a lot about extreme hardship, proving extreme hardship and getting the favorable discretion. I hear a lot of people say you just need an assessment from a counselor and that's the magic ticket. You get assessed psychologically and they say you're stressed out because of the separation, and so that's how you get the waiver. Or people sometimes say it depends on the U.S. citizen's statement or letter that you write and it has to prove everything and that's how you get the waiver. Or they talk about different discretionary factors and think that one particular thing is going to totally disqualify the person, or in a lot of cases people think the waivers only depend on the discretionary factors so they'll just think, "Okay, all I have to do is get a big stack of letters saying my husband's an awesome guy." I'm sure he is an awesome guy, because that's why you married him, but that's not everything that you need to show and it's not going to be enough for these waivers.

The waivers really do involve lots of different types of evidence and it's going to be really important to really prove those different factors to a higher degree and to make it personal. There's no easy answer, like you just go to the psychologist and they say you're anxious and depressed and so you're good to go. It's going to be really a customized, personal thing for every client.

That's a little bit about what we're actually showing on the waivers, you know, what are we actually putting on these applications, what do you actually have to show to win your waiver.

Now I want to talk about the two main ways, or the two main procedures that we have to use to get people waivers. We'll talk about the mechanics and the logistics of actually getting the waivers. There are two main ways I would say that we usually see. For most people who are doing an adjustment of status in the United States as we discussed earlier, they actually typically don't need waivers because they're avoiding the whole unlawful presence problem because they don't have to leave the United States and trigger the bars. If they qualify for adjustment of status they're not going to have a problem with unlawful presence because they're still in the United States so we can avoid that whole issue.

In theory if they have other types of grounds of inadmissibility like maybe fraud or something like that, you can file waivers with the adjustment of status but it's just not very common that we see that. We're really not going to go into that, but I did want to mention that that option does exist in immigration law.

The two main ways that we get waivers though, because most

of the waivers we do are for undocumented presence and then sometimes additional issues. We help a lot of people who have to go back to their home country to do the interview. So the waivers come into play when we're doing those types of cases and doing what's called consular processing, which means that they have to do part of the case going abroad to their embassy and doing an interview before they come back into the United States as residents.

Traditionally what would happen is you would start a marriage petition in the United States. You would prove that you had a real relationship, that it was valid, wasn't just a fake marriage you did to get somebody papers. They would approve that phase, and then they would have to get set up the interview abroad. The immigrant would travel abroad. They would have the interview and the officer would say, "Okay well you're inadmissible because you've been in the United States undocumented, or you're inadmissible because whatever," and they would tell the person why they were inadmissible. Once they did that, the immigrant would be able to submit the application for the waiver.

Of course lawyers would know about the problem ahead of time, right, and would be preparing the waiver ahead of time so that as soon as the officer said "you're inadmissible," they would say "great, here's my waiver application" and try to get it approved. The problem was it wasn't something they would look at right then. It was something that would go into a big pile. There'd be other officers that had to look at it. It could take months or even years to get a decision. If the person didn't win their waiver, they would be stuck outside of the country for who knows how long, in some cases it would be 10 years, right, that they could be stuck out of the country. If they didn't win the waiver there's no way for them to legally get back in.

It was really a tough decision for a lot of families to make because it's the only way for them, or it was previously the only way for some people to get their green card through the marriage but it was at such a huge risk that people were hesitant, obviously, to try that. Many people did, many people didn't. The important and good part of this story is that there's another option available for at least some of those people now, and that is currently what the most common procedure that we're doing. It's called a provisional waiver.

What happened is, fortunately, the Obama administration looked at this problem and said "okay how can we do something to improve this situation." Although the president can't just change the laws, there're some administrative type office processing policies that the president does have control over. What they started doing was allowing people to apply for their waiver while they were still in the United States.

What you do first, you still have to do a petition, prove that your marriage is real, your relationship is legit, and then you can apply for your waiver while you're still inside the United States. If they grant the waiver, you get what's called a conditional approval. That means you've got your waiver, granted, in your pocket before you go to your interview abroad. You still have to go abroad, still have to do the interview, but you basically know that you've already won your case by the time you leave. That's great because if people don't win their waiver for whatever reason, they just simply don't leave the country. Unless they're terrorists or something they aren't going after the people who don't win the waivers. So people really have that security where they can apply and see if they're going to win and almost all the risk is gone for them.

If they win they waiver then all they have to do is go to the interview and as long as there's nothing huge that they didn't mention, that they lied about, or something that comes up, you know another ground of inadmissibility, then they're good to go. They do their medical exam, they do their interview, they come back in as residents.

Obviously, people who qualify for that are thrilled about that and we're just thrilled that that's an option right now. One thing that's a big drawback or a big caveat to that particular program is that it can only be for people who need waivers for unlawful presence and nothing else.

Some people need waivers for things we've mentioned like fraud or misrepresentation, or maybe they need criminal waivers, or maybe they have a deportation order or they have other issues, they're not going to be able to use the provisional waiver program, at least as it stands today. So for some people we have to discuss general strategy, whether they want to go the traditional route or whether it makes sense to do some other maneuvers first so that they can qualify for that provisional waiver route.

As you are Googling and learning more about the procedures, that's the difference between those two methods of processing. I hope that makes sense, and certainly that's something where you'd want to get advice about which one you might qualify for, and it's always, always, always, always super important to remember to never leave the United States before you are sure what your strategy is. Sometimes people will start these cases and they just kind of follow the chain of documents. "Great, we got our petition approved. Now they sent us papers saying sign up for your interview abroad." For whatever reason, the couple doesn't contact a lawyer until after they're abroad and they realize that they're inadmissible. At that point it's unfortunate because there's was a much better process that they could have followed to prevent having to spent months or longer outside the U.S. Or in some cases there is no waiver for their ground of inadmissibility or maybe no waiver that they can apply for until 10 years have passed, and that puts them and their family in a very difficult situation.

Really the government is not going to look at your case and tell you what the best option is. They're not lawyers and they're not on your side, so it wouldn't really make sense for them to do that. They just send you notifications as you reach the end of different steps in the process. They aren't going to tell you you're about to walk off a cliff. It's not to say they are mean-spirited about it; it's just not their role in the process. They simply try to determine legally whether each person who sends an application or shows up at an interview legally should be granted whatever they have asked for. Please, before you leave the country, always, always, always figure out what's the best route for you to personally take.

That kind of sums up what I wanted to talk about tonight. We've talked about the basic types of things we usually see waived. What types of things you have to show to actually get the waiver; extreme hardship, discretionary factors. Then the two main procedures that we're currently using to get people waivers through their marriage, which is the traditional route, and also the more recently enacted provisional waiver program.

I'm not sure if there are any questions out there but I wanted to pass this over to Megan so that she can explain how to ask questions if you do have them. Please remember that this is being recorded; it will be available to the public, so don't go into too much personal detail, but if you have general questions then please feel free to go ahead and I'll do my best to answer and clarify any issues that you may have had. Megan, why don't you take it over?

Megan: Absolutely. For those of you who have questions, just go ahead and press *6 on your phone now and that'll put you into the cue. As soon as I see that you have a question I'll say the last four digits of your phone number so you'll know that your line has been unmuted and then you can go ahead with your question. As Clare said, this is being recorded, so when you introduce yourself just use your first name only and like she said don't go into too much detail for your privacy.

Okay, let's go ahead to our first caller now. Caller with the last four digits 0200. 0200 your line has just been unmuted and you can go ahead with your question.

Caller: Oh hi, thank you very much. My name is Rita but my question is actually about a friend of mine. He has already been to see some lawyers but the lawyers told him that his wife can't apply for him because he has come into the US illegally twice and that there's no way to fix that. Did you say that there is some kind of waiver for that problem too?

Clare: Yeah, that's actually a great question; I'm glad you asked that to kind of clarify a point about what we discussed. It is true that there is a ground of inadmissibility that applies to some people because they've entered the United States twice without documents both times. It doesn't apply to everyone who's entered the United States twice, it depends on the years that they came and went and the amount of time between their entries. There are a lot of details. First of all, you'd want to make sure that it actually applies to him.

If he's gone to good reputable immigration lawyers, they probably have analyzed that correctly, I assume. If that ground of inadmissibility does apply to him, a lot of times people will call that penalty "the permanent bar," which is the slang on the street. I don't like that terminology because technically, it's not actually permanent. The reason they call it the permanent bar is that if you don't get a waiver for it eventually, there's no period of time abroad that will just erase the problem. That's different from the 3 and 10-year bars, where an immigrant can stay outside of the United States for that period of time, and the bar will expire at the end of that time period. After that time is up, they don't need a waiver to apply with their spouse and get a green card.

But so in the case of an immigrant who is subject to the so-called "permanent bar," the waiver that's available for people with that issue, assuming of course that this does apply to him, is that he would have to first leave the United States for ten whole years and then his wife could apply for the waiver to get him back in. If she didn't obtain the waiver, then he would continue to have the bar, even after spending 10 years abroad. The issue doesn't go away until he gets the waiver. That's why people sometimes call it the permanent bar. That's why some lawyers will say there's nothing you can do in this case. I personally take the approach that I want my clients to understand the truth and then make the best decision for their family based on that information.

People typically do not want to take that option and go abroad for 10 years and then try to get back in, but it is an important distinction, like you said, to say whether or not there's a waiver available. It's different if you just don't want to do that right now and you're waiting for better options, versus there's actually no way you can do it.

There's another sort of wrinkle in that analysis which is there are waivers available for that same situation under different programs. For some couples like that, I'll see that and it's like, "Hey, that's your only option through a marriage immigration case, but actually you qualify for this other thing such as a crime victim visa that does give you a waiver for that and you don't have to go out for 10 years to get that waiver." It's always an overall analysis, but you're right for some people when that applies to them they're not willing to go through that process to get the waiver and they don't currently have any other options either, You know, I do have the hope that that's something that's going to improve in the future, through a lot of lobbying efforts and I am hoping and pushing for Congress to change the law to give us a better waiver for that particular issue, or somehow lessen that burden on people.

If you've got any questions about that, I'd be happy to talk with your friend. Have him make a consultation. Certainly do make sure that he's been talking with people who practice immigration law exclusively and that they do work with a lot of waivers and a lot of married couples specifically before he gives up hope. Back before I was a lawyer and we were going through the ordeal with my husband, we had three supposed immigration lawyers tell us that there was absolutely nothing that could be done in his case, before we found the lawyer who fixed everything for us. At the same time, everyone should be very careful and not necessarily trust a person who says something can be done when other lawyers have advised against taking action. There are scam artists out there who take advantage of couples in tough situations. Or sometimes lawyers who have good intentions but aren't up to date on the nuances of immigration law.

Hopefully that, does that clarify the question?

Caller: I don't really know who he's talked to, but your information has been so helpful. I'll pass that along to him. Thank you.

Clare: Great, and you know these recordings are going to be available after we finish with all the five classes, so you could also pass the recordings on to him as well to kind of give him some more direction.

Caller: Should he just call your office to get those recordings?

Clare: He can do that, sure, or email. Our email is office@coradolaw.

com and we can send him the recordings that way. We also will probably post them on our website and put them on iTunes as podcasts because sometimes that is more convenient for people.

Caller: Well, thank you so much.

Clare: You're welcome, have a good evening.

Megan: Thanks for that question. Do we have any other questions? Again, all you have to do is press *6. I'll give everybody a couple seconds in case they are thinking of their question. I see we have another question here. The last four digits of the phone number is 0189. 0189 go ahead with your question.

Makeen: Hi yes my name is Makeen, and I am from Dubai. I have a question, if I am going to start a waiver case, how do I know how likely it is to work?

Clare: That's a great question, and it's something that people definitely ask me a lot and it's obviously very important to your decisions. The thing about waivers is it's sometimes hard to know whether they're going to be granted or not. What I like to do with people is to talk through their personal situation and figure out how strong their arguments are so we can give them a better idea. From experience I can give them a better idea of how likely it is that they will get the waiver, or whether they should maybe wait for whatever reason.

Another thing that's going to be really important to you as you're deciding if you want to try for a waiver or not is which option you qualify for. For people who can get a provisional waiver, they're really not having very much risk to trying their case. Even if they're not sure if they can get the waiver or they don't have a particularly wonderful case, a lot of them will say, "Well, when you look at the benefits of getting a green card, I'm going to try and go for it." But then they would, if they had to leave the country and risk it that way they would be less likely to do it.

I think that's going to be an important thing for any particular person to consider when they're deciding. But yes, without having a very detailed conversation with you about that or with the person you're asking about it's something I really can't say. It's going to depend on all the factors we talked about, about the hardships, the discretionary factors, and exactly what the ground of inadmissibility is. Does that make sense?

Yes, it does. Thank you very much. What is the phone number of your office so I can call in and see if we can make a consultation?

Clare: Sure, our number is 317-247-5040. Or you can always email at the email I gave earlier, office@coradolaw.com Either one is fine. Or Google us and go to our website.

Caller: Okay, thank you very much.

Clare: You're welcome, have a nice evening.

Megan: Okay, do we have any other questions? Just *6 is all you have to press and I'll see you have a question. Again, I'll give everybody a couple more seconds just in case we have one last question. I'm not seeing any more questions. I know that a lot of you might not want to ask your questions online because it is personal, so again just feel free to contact our office and set up a meeting with someone at our office and we can analyze your situation and help you to best understand the options you have for your particular case.

Like I mentioned earlier, we'll be sending out all of these records from all five classes to you a few days after our last class. Also please join us tomorrow night for our fourth class. It will be at 7PM again and Clare will be talking about a hugely important topic: How to plan your wedding and life around complicated immigration timelines. I'm sure that's something that all of you will want to know. Take care and we'll see you then. Good night.

Part 4 – How to Plan Around Tricky Immigration Timelines

Megan: Okay, it's 7:00. Good evening everyone. We'll go ahead and get started. Welcome to our fourth call in this series. I'm Megan, and I'll be hosting tonight's call with Immigration Attorney Clare Corado. Those of you who have been joining us throughout this series already know that Clare is the lawyer who loves to work with married and engaged couples, in helping them build their lives together in the United States.

               Tonight's topic is how to plan around tricky Immigration timelines. This is a great topic. Before we get started, I just wanted to let you know that this call will be recorded, and all the recordings will be available, just like the other ones have been. Claire, are you ready to take it from here?

Clare: Yes, I am, Megan. Thank you. You know, I'm really excited to be talking about this. It's a really great topic. This is one of those things that you don't necessarily find a lot of information about online. It is something that is crucial when you're planning your case. The timing really affects everything else that you're planning. People, when they come to see me, they're right in the middle of planning their weddings, and their honeymoons, and international travel. Thinking about when their fiancé or spouse is going to start working in the US. When they're going to do the move. When they're going to get the relatives to come over and visit. All of those details depend on the timing of the Immigration case.

               One of the especially tricky things for couples who are going through the Immigration process is that there's no set timeframe for the cases. I can give people a general average, but it's going to vary for any particular person. We really never know which cases are going to be the ones that are going to have a lot of random surprises that put us behind schedule. Sometimes we even have the surprise of things going through a lot faster than we expected. That's a good problem to have, but sometimes it really throws a wrench into things.

Today, we're going to talk about some good ways you can cope with that variability, and set some things up to be, hopefully, the least stressful way possible. This topic, I want to mention, it's one part of a couple's experience that I really used to overlook. We don't think of it in the traditional way of being part of the legal case. As I was talking to clients over time, and people continually brought it up in the consultation, I really started to realize that this wedding planning, this planning of their time-line, is actually a really crucial part of the problem that they're wanting us to solve.

It's our job to make their life better, make their Immigration experience easier. Now, I actually start my first meeting with new clients with these kind of questions. What are your ideal plans? How would you be doing your wedding, and your reception, and your honeymoon if you were already both US citizens and the Immigration issue weren't on the table? When would be the ideal time to move to the US? Is there anything you'd take care of in your home country before you can move here? A lot of people need to graduate, or wrap up some other issue they have in their country, before they can actually move to the United States.

Based on the information they give me at that point, we make a time-line, and start brainstorming how we can possibly approach their case strategy. How we can manage their case flow in the best possible way, considering their preferences. Or, at least, to try to get them the most important things that they want, and still fit it all into the time-frame of an Immigration case. With Immigration law, it's always an adventure, for sure.

The number one, super-number-one rule of Immigration planning is that the time-lines will change. You really never want to get into a position where you absolutely have to have something happen by a certain date. It's just a very risky thing to do. Please, whatever you do, don't make big commitments that you can't get out of if the timing doesn't work out as you are hoping that it will work out. I don't know if I believe in jinxes, but you're asking to have problems. It's just so unpredictable, so you want to be very aware of that.

There are a few different reasons people wonder what's the average case time. They always seem surprised that even an Immigration lawyer can't tell them for sure how long the case will take. I wanted to cover some of the factors that we see that are really out of our control, that can cause your case to take longer, in some cases, even significantly longer than the average case.

Sometimes, after the cases get submitted, and there are several phases of the cases typically, at certain phases, the government may request more documents. Sometimes that happens even if all the required documents were sent from the beginning, which you know if you work with a lawyer, everything required will be sent at the beginning of the phase. Sometimes they ask for other things, or they're not satisfied with what was sent. Sometimes those requests put the time-line behind, kind of put you back in line.

Another type of delay we see a lot is something that is absolutely completely out of your control, which is an increase of applications filed by other people. You never really know when there are going to be surges in everybody filing their Immigration case. Even certain times of year, or for whatever reason, more people in a certain area of the world might be filing applications. If their workload increases and their staffing doesn't, then it's just going to slow down a little bit. We see variations because of that. It's basically unpredictable when that happens.

Another thing that we see sometimes is changes in government procedures that happen in the middle of your case. It may be ... The cases sometimes last nine months, a year, a year and a half, even two years, depending on what the process is that we're doing for a particular client. Sometimes we're half-way through and then we realize that there's going to be a change in the way a certain phase is processed. That would definitely be one advantage, actually, to working with a lawyer. We are already testing out that changed process with other clients, usually, by the time your change happens. We're already dealing with it, so you don't get as much of a big surprise. For everyone, even the government processing in a new way, it always has a few kinks that need worked out when that happens.

We also see, sometimes, technology problems. For example, even in this past year, there was a problem with one of the major computer systems for one of the processing phases for people who do their interviews in US Consulates overseas. For people who are doing Consular Processing, one of the interim offices has a computer system that you have to go through. It actually went down for a few weeks. It's absolutely crucial to that step. It was very difficult. It put some cases behind. They actually made a work-around method by paper, so we were all trying to do it a different way. It was really interesting. Fortunately, it got resolved eventually, and those cases went through. That certainly was an unexpected delay that we saw in those cases.

There can also be problems with mail. We occasionally see, even with the well-known mail carriers, people send ... It ends up on the wrong continent occasionally. If somebody enters a code in wrong at your mailing company. Sometimes that makes a slight delay. Obviously, that's very rare, but we have seen some funny ones before. I think we saw one that it was supposed to go somewhere in Europe, and the country name started with the same letter as some place in South America. It ended up in completely the wrong place.

Another problem that we do see that is a little bit more common is difficulty obtaining certain types of documents from certain parts of the world. There are definitely some countries where certain public record type legal documents can be harder to get. Sometimes, we're sending somebody's fiancé or spouse to some remote mountain village so they can get the exact thing that we're asking for. Sometimes that takes a little bit of leg-work. That certainly can be something difficult, but if you're working with a lawyer, someone who knows how to do these types of cases, they'll be able to tell you what those documents would be up front, so that you can get started ahead of time, getting the hardest to get things that are going to be foreseeably difficult in your case.

It can be really frustrating for a lot of people to know that so many of those factors are actually out of their control. The most important thing to remember is that the most common factors that actually cause our cases to take longer, actually are under the control of the client. For clients who are really on it, and they want to finish as soon as possible, they want to get everything in order, there are a lot of things they can do to make that happen.

The first thing I would recommend absolutely is, as soon as you realize this is going to be a possibility, you're engaged, maybe you're even thinking about getting engaged to someone who does not have ... Who is not a US citizen or resident, you should get advice about your case, so that you can understand what the time-lines will look like. Almost all the people who consult with us are already too close to their preferred wedding date. They don't realize how long it's really going to take. They think, "Well, three months is plenty of time, or six months." It would always benefit them to have gotten advice earlier on in the process, so they could decide what the strategy was going to be, get started, get a lawyer fast, and just start getting everything in order. That would be the first thing that would absolutely help you get it done faster.

The second thing would be collect all your personal documents, your relationship documents that your lawyer requests as soon as possible. The time can pass pretty quickly, getting stuff together, it's just an errand or chore that people have to do. Time can really slip away when you're in that process. Definitely make a personal commitment to yourself to get that stuff together quickly so that all the delay is on Immigration's side, and not on your side.

Then, also, just be sure to stay in contact with your lawyer and the paralegal at the law office you're working with, and respond to any request of theirs as soon as possible. Any time something's missing, or maybe the government has asked for something else that needs to be submitted, it won't be able to be submitted until they have the information they need. For clients who are really quick to respond, quick to get those things that we need, they completely minimize the delays on our side. That's definitely a good thing. You're always going to have to wait for the Immigration side, but for the side you can control, if you want it to go faster, you can definitely do your part to make that happen.

Aside from the different ways that it can ... We talked about ways that things can get delayed, and ways that you can help them go a little bit faster. There are some other issues that have to do more with the tactics of where the wedding happens, where the honeymoon happens, when it happens. We've discovered over time that there are patterns of tactics that are commonly used, or sometimes combined in the different cases, that can help you deal with the time-line and the headache issues that we see in Immigration cases.

I'm going to go through several of those tactics that I see most commonly. Then take some questions, if you have them. Hopefully, this will get your wheels spinning about what might work in your case, what might be a strategic way to do what you need to do, and work still within the time-frame of your Immigration case.

The first tactic we see is for some people to ... This is applicable mostly when people are expecting to get a Fiancé Visa. Just like we talked about in the very first call, some people, their fiancé is living abroad, and they're going to get a visa to bring that person into the United States. They don't know exactly the timing of the visa, but once the person comes to the United States, they only have 90 days to get married. It's hard to plan the wedding not knowing exactly when they'll be there. Then you have to pull off a fast wedding at that time.

Some people who really want to have a nice wedding, and do everything at that wedding, but they're waiting on that unknown time-frame, what they'll do is, they'll get everything mostly done, I guess I would say, for the wedding. Then have everything on hold and just waiting, so they can trigger their plan on short notice, and still get all the pieces together. For these types of plans, we have some wedding planners we actually work with who are great at doing this, because it's their profession, obviously. That can be a good option. Even if you're not going to get help with the organizing of the wedding, these are some things that you can do yourself, as well.

You might want to choose a venue that you don't have to reserve far in advance. Especially popular are, if you know somebody with a nice house, a nice backyard, a park that doesn't require any sort of special reservation or signing up for having your wedding there. Those can be good options. Someplace that you can book quickly for actually holding the wedding or the reception. Or, you can choose a few places that sometimes do have last-minute openings. As soon as you know the wedding is going to happen soon, you would call all of them and see who might have a spot for the particular dates that you're looking at.

As far as your decorations, you can make or buy decorations that can be stored until needed. Maybe, candles instead of flowers. Things like that that can be prepared ahead of time, and just be held in waiting for that moment when you actually go ahead and pull off the wedding. There are other things you can get up to the mostly-done standard, like having every-thing set up for your invitations. Ready to be printed or to be sent electronically, as soon as you fill in the date, once you confirm that. You can talk with multiple vendors for different categories of things that you're going to need, like a photog-rapher, DJ, or cake vendor, so that you have a list of potential different people to call, once you know the date. You might have three photographers that are potential, so that once you know the time, you just start calling the ones you've already screened to see who might be available.

You're also definitely going to want to find out what the marriage license requirements are in your county ahead of time, so you can be sure to get that as soon as possible, once you're ready. That varies by county, even if not even a state-wide thing. You definitely want to go ahead and ask them that ahead of time, and just see exactly what you need, so you don't have any delay there, if you're trying to pull off the wedding quickly.

As far as somebody to actually perform the wedding, if you

don't have a particular person you would want to officiate, usually people who have some sort of religious practice will use a minister or whatever their religious celebrant would be. If you're not sure, or don't have a particular person in mind, there are companies that actually have access to many people who are able to officiate a wedding. Typically, they would be able to get you an officiant more quickly, last-minute on your particular chosen day. You might want to make a relationship with a company like that. We do have some connections to groups like that, as well, if that's something that you need.

That first tactic is, "Get everything mostly done, and then hold on it until the date comes up and you're ready to go. Then you just pull the trigger and try to pull all the details together." The second tactic that we see people go for is to do all the legal paperwork first, then to have your big dream wedding or reception once it's all done. You basically are going to focus on the Immigration side of things, and then later on you're going to have your big party.

What those plans require would just be having a legal ceremony only. A civil ceremony. Just going to the courthouse type wedding, or something small. Then, they typically start planning their ... It's usually a reception or something with their families, to actually happen after residence. It's something they would allow themselves the normal planning time. I believe from my wedding planner contacts, that people right now are usually taking 12 to 18 months to plan a wedding, the traditional average. People who choose this tactic would have their green card in hand, or be very close. They would start planning a year or year and a half out, so they're sure they would get through the process by then, and that won't be an issue at all.

That can be great for people who have a very definite idea of how they want everything to go down with the ceremony ore reception part of the party. If they really have particular desire to have a party with certain details, or certain relatives there, some things that are very specific, that can be a great way for them not to have to stress about the time-line. To be sure that they can do the details exactly how they want them to be done. Another thing that is nice about that is, it enables both spouses to be in the US, to be working in the US by the time they get around to actually having this party. It helps with the expenses, as well, so that everybody's already established and working by the time they would get to that point.

Some of the drawbacks to that particular tactic would be a lot of people don't want to separate their legal wedding and their church wedding, or their legal wedding and their party. That's understandable. For some people that's not even an option they would consider. Just tradition, or personal preference. Another drawback is, you'd be delaying it a long time, if you have a longer type green card case, realistically, your party might be three years after your legal marriage. Assuming if you do the entire case, and then you plan your wedding out after that, another year and a half. It can be quite far away from the actual ceremony. For some people, that just wouldn't be the same.

Another thing to watch out for this one, if there are some details of your relationship or your wedding that are already potential red flags for Immigration, having a small, civil, legal ceremony without any type of party, or without any type of celebration, could actually hurt your case in some instances. It just looks like a less legitimate relationship. I would say, don't freak out about that and think this isn't an option for you just because you don't want to hurt your case. That would not be true for everyone. An Immigration lawyer who does marriage cases would be able to talk with you about your personal circumstances and advise you about whether or not that would be okay to take this option in your case. It definitely is something to consider.

The third tactic that we see a lot is for people who are unable to leave the country after their wedding, because they're waiting on their Adjustment of Status to go through. A quick review of the options we talked about. There's the option of getting a Fiancé Visa coming to the United States, then applying for your green card here. Then, some people are already in the United States for some reason, on another type of work visa, or something like that. They also do an Adjustment of Status process in the United States. One of the limitations on them is that they can't travel abroad after that until they've either received a travel permit, which usually takes at least 90 days, or gotten their actual green card. They're kind of stuck here for a few months.

For some people, their ideal honeymoon is really going to be something abroad. They kind of had an idea they were going to go to some particular place, and that's something that's going to be difficult because they have to stay put right after the wedding, at least for several months while their case goes through. A lot of people will choose to honeymoon inside the United States, if they have their hearts set on having the honeymoon right after the wedding. We've actually got a lot of great options in the United States. It's a nice, big country.

Some people, instead of the classic, "We're going to the Caribbean, or going to a Mexican beach," they'll instead go for Hawaii, they'll go to Niagara Falls. Maybe just a little cabin out in Wyoming in the wilderness, or some kind of gorgeous beach in California, or Florida, or somewhere in the mountains. There are actually a lot of nice options in the US. A lot of people will go for that option. Maybe save their dream trip abroad for a celebration after they get through the green card process, or for their anniversary, or some future date. That can always be an option if you're not willing to save your honeymoon until after the green card case is done.

The fourth tactic that we see in that people in some cases will separate the religious ceremony from the civil ceremony, or the actual legal ceremony. In a lot of places abroad, you can actually do that. It's much less common in the United States to be able to separate your religious and your legal ceremonies. Although we have seen it definitely be possible. The reason that someone would do this would be because if you have the religious ceremony only abroad, then you're not legally married. That still gives you the option to get a Fiancé Visa to come over, because you're still a fiancé. Then finish the legal part of it in the United States.

People will choose that option if they want to have their big party abroad. Maybe if there are a lot of family members abroad, and the travel planning would be difficult for them. They'll hold their big religious, or just their party, abroad. Then they'll come to the United States and finish things up. You just want to be extra, extra, super-duper sure that wherever you're holding that celebration at, you're not technically entering into a marriage. There are countries where just having a religious ceremony could actually cause you to be legally married under the country's laws. You definitely want to investigate that if that's something you're leaning towards. Keep that in mind that that is a possibility to actually do that.

The fifth tactic I wanted to cover is that some people decide to go a different route. Instead of the Fiancé Visa, for example, they'll say, "We want to have our religious ceremony or party together with our civil ceremony. We want to do it all abroad all at one time. We want to have control over the timing." For people with that preference, it's typically better for them to do Consular Processing, which is the case we do after the person's already your spouse. Or, a K-3 Visa, which is another way to bring in a spouse into the United States.

The benefit of that would just be you get to do your own planning on your own timing. Typically, American relatives here have a little easier time traveling to most countries. Americans aren't really required to get visas for as many countries as some other countries are to come to the United States. It might be just an easier planning time to do everything abroad, and then bring your spouse in. The huge drawback to that one is just that it really stinks to go get married abroad, have this wonderful party, maybe even your honeymoon, and then come back to the US alone after the wedding, and wait several months to get your spouse in. People really hate that, understandably. That's definitely something to keep in mind when you're deciding what route you want to go through.

The next tactic I wanted to discuss is some people will, if they've come to consult with a lawyer with plenty of time, we can actually start the process with extra time. We'll see this in a lot of Fiancé Visa cases where we know the general average time that it's taking to do a Fiancé Visa under the current numbers. I'm not even going to say what the current time is, because I don't know when people are listening to this recording. I'm sure it will have changed by then. It changes every day, basically. We will look at the time, and say, "Based on the current timing, we could get you a Fiancé Visa even before you are ready to move to the United States, or you're ready to finish up whatever you have to do in your country."

We'll start anyway, early, because we know we can get the case almost completely done, and to stall at a few of the last steps, so that we know that some of the variable time-frames, or the potential problems we will have already passed that part of the case. We can just keep it in a holding pattern until we get closer to the exact date that they want. Then with the Fiancé Visa, you typically have six months to actually enter the US after it's been issued. We'll stall for enough time until we get them into that window, then complete the process. That gives them a lot more control over the timing. Of course, to take that route, you have to have come earlier than what you needed. For that reason, it's not as common as I would like to see, actually. That would be a really good option for a lot of people. That, of course, depends on when you actually want to come.

A lot of people also just want to come as soon as possible. They don't, maybe, have anything to wrap up in their home country. They would just want to go through as quickly as possible anyway.

The next tactic that we see sometimes is when the US spouse spends time abroad, so there's no separation. If the US spouse can ... Or fiancé, can move their job, or maybe they have a distance job, or they can afford to not work for a few months, they can just pick up and go live abroad. Assuming that they've got everything in line with the foreign country. I'm definitely not an Immigration lawyer for other countries. It's something we can help people find the resources needed investigate, like the contact info of the foreign Embassy, but obviously not advise them about: how to become a permanent resident in the UK, or in Canada, or anywhere else. Permanent residence or whatever they call it there; actually they probably don't even call it that. People can sometimes spend some of that time together abroad, instead of having to be separated the whole time. Which is one of the toughest parts of an Immigration case, being physically separated for a long time.

When people do that, it works pretty well. The only thing that makes it a little bit complicated or something that you have to consider is that the American citizen does have to prove that they intend to move back to the United States with their spouse. People will occasionally ... We'll see cases abroad where they want to move the foreign spouse into the United

States, and the US spouse has things to finish up in the foreign country, and they don't plan on going with them in the beginning. That's actually not allowed. You have to both be ready to go back to the United States and to show that, if that's the option you want to take, if you're going to spend some time abroad.

The final tactic I wanted to cover is a reflection, a variation, of the one that we just discussed, except it works the opposite way. In some cases, it might be possible for the foreign fiancé or spouse to spend some time in the US while the case is pending. Now, this one, I have to say is super-tricky. It only works for people who have some other type of visa already in the United States. Sometimes we'll see people who have a tourist visa, or some kind of student visa. Some way that they can travel in and out of the United States. They're able to come in, visit for several months. We'll start the case processing then. Of course, always with the intention of going back to their home country to finish the process. As we discussed earlier, it's considered visa fraud to come in with a temporary, a non-Immigrant visa, like a tourist visa, with the intention to get married and stay in the United States.

The good thing is, it's actually legally fine to come in temporarily intending to visit while your case starts processing. The problem with that tactic ... I want to put a lot of asterisks behind this one ... It's actually much harder to enter the United States with a tourist visa if you have a girlfriend or a fiancé or a spouse here, and especially if you've already started the case. Immigration is going to look at it very suspiciously, thinking that this person actually does want to commit visa fraud, and they're just going to stay. In some cases, you have to be aware that there is the risk that the person might come to visit intending to try to spend some time here while things are processing. They could even be turned away at Customs.

I would not try that tactic, or any version of it without the help of a lawyer. It is something that we have been able to carefully plan for some couples, and actually pull off to limit their time separated. Which is just awesome. I did want to mention it as a possible tactic to ask your lawyer about, if it might apply to you.

Now that we've thrown a lot of different ideas out there, and everybody's case is going to be different, for sure. Maybe that brought up some ideas about what could be done, so I wanted to just open this up for questions to see if anyone has anything to ask. You can feel free to ask about today's topic, or anything that we've discussed in the series so far, or other Immigration questions. I'm happy to answer if there's anything out there. Just go for it. Megan, are you ready?

Megan: Yes, I've just opened the Q&A session now. If any of you need to ask questions, all you have to do is press *6 to raise your hand, and I'll see you have a question. All you need to say is just your first name, since this is being recorded, for privacy purposes. I'll say the last four digits of your phone number, and then you'll know your line has been unmuted, and you can go ahead with your question. I'll give everybody a couple seconds. Again, just *6.

Okay, again, if you have a question, it's just star-6. Okay, thanks, 0576, go ahead with your question. The individual who has the last four digits of their phone number is 0576, go ahead with your question.

Caller: Hi, thanks. How would I know if my church would let us do the civil and religious ceremonies separately?

Clare: That's a great question. It's really something that we have to investigate in every case. Typically, we would start by asking some religious leader in your church. If you're thinking of doing the wedding abroad, ask abroad. The interesting thing that we've found is that some churches will not do it in the United States, but abroad they will. For example, we've done a lot of couples who are getting married through the Catholic Church. Here in the United States, at least in the cases that we've seen, the Catholic Church has been unwilling to actually marry people, for example, through a mass or an actual religious ceremony without carrying out the legal wedding in the United States as well. However, it's extremely common that they will do the Catholic and legal ceremonies separately for you in Latin America. It's going to depend on your particular religion, your particular church. It's something you have to investigate in every case. I would start by asking your religious leader if that might be possible.

Caller: Great, okay. Thanks a lot.

Clare: Yeah. Good luck.

Caller: Thanks.

Megan: Okay, for anyone else who has a question, all you have to do is press *6 to raise your hand, then I'll say the last four digits of your phone number. You'll be able to go ahead with your question. Okay, I see we have another question here. The individual with the phone number with the last four digits 3991, 3991, go ahead with your question.

Caller: Hello, Clare. Thank you so much for your advice. I am wondering if red flags in cases, if you could explain that more ...

Clare: Yeah, I think I had mentioned that briefly earlier. You mean when I was talking about people who maybe should not consider doing just a quick at the courthouse ceremony? Is that what you mean?

Caller: Yes. Can you explain that a little bit more?

Clare: Yeah, absolutely. Immigration actually has some things that
          they look for, because they're always trying to figure out
          whether people really have a relationship, whether they're
          really in love, and want to stay together and start a lifetime
          together. Or if it's just a scam to get Immigration documents.
          There's actually an interesting list that's out there that some-
          body somehow discovered that was a list that they called
          Fraud Indicators. They'll look more closely at certain cases
          that differ from what their stereotypical idea of what a rela-
          tionship looks like.

          Say somebody was dating a very short time, and then they
          got married. Or, say the person has a big difference in age. Or,
          maybe they have a difference in their religions that they prac-
          tice, or they don't speak a common language very well. Things
          like that are on the list. It's not to say that those things would
          prevent you from being able to do your case. It's just that if
          you already have a lot of those things going on, or some other
          details that make it more difficult, I wouldn't want you to
          complicate the situation by also having a wedding that didn't
          look very serious. Which in some cases, they can interpret it
          that way, if you've got other issues. I would say, if any of those
          things sound like, "That might apply to me," or you're just cu-
          rious, please contact our office and we would be happy to talk
          you through that. It's something we'd want to go through all
          the details and I'd want to decide in my professional opinion
          how risky the case was. Or whether you could go ahead and
          do that.

          You should definitely also listen to the last class that we're go-
          ing to have next week. We're going to talk about the marriage
          interview. I'm going to go into a lot more detail about what
          types of things they're looking for, and what types of things
          might be red flags. Be sure to catch that one, too.

Caller: Thank you.

Clare: You're welcome.

Megan: Okay. I see that we have some other callers on the line. I will give you all a couple more seconds, just in case you have a question. Again, just press *6 raise your hand. Okay, it looks like we don't have any more questions, and that was our last question for tonight. Hopefully, all of this information helped to clear up a lot of the questions you may have had before the session. Be sure to put the date on your calendar of our final call in the series. It's going to be next Tuesday at 7:00 pm, Eastern time. This topic's going to be a fun one, as well. It's about the marriage interview. Clare will be discussing how the interviews really work, and what is just urban legend.

For people who call into this final call for the series, we will be sending a bonus of Clare's List of the Most Common Questions Asked at Marriage Interviews. I know you won't want to miss that. If you have friends who might be going through an Immigration case as well, please feel free to invite them to the last call. Just be sure they sign up with us personally, by calling our phone number. It's 317-247-5040. Or, they can also email us at office@Coradolaw.com. Then, we'll send them all the bonus materials, as well. Even if they haven't tuned in until now, they will still have access to the previous recordings from all four of these sessions, and then also for the last session. They can get the info from the entire series of classes.

We look forward to seeing you on our last call next Tuesday. I hope everyone has a good evening. Good-bye.

Part 5 – The Marriage Interview: Truth vs Urban Legend

Megan: Good evening everyone, and welcome to our final call in this series. It's 7:00 so we'll go ahead and get started. I'm Megan and I'll be hosting tonight's call with immigration attorney Clare Corado. We've covered a lot of ground in the past few weeks, and we're going to top it off with a really fun topic, The Marriage Interview: Truth vs. Urban Legend.

Let's go ahead and make sure Clare is on the call and ready to go. Clare are you there?

Clare: Yep, I'm here. Thanks, Megan. I'm so excited to be able to discuss all this information with you. We're on our very last call; we've covered a ton. It was very exciting. Thanks for all of your comments and even some suggestions of future topics that we could do. So, we're probably going to try to set up some more of these calls. I want to talk tonight about one of my favorite topics in immigration law, because there is just so much cultural mystique about the marriage interview at the immigration office.

You see it in a lot of movies and on TV. Nobody really knows what happens, and everybody's a little bit afraid of it. Of course you read lots of things online that are just hilarious, or totally crazy. It's just a question I get a lot and I just think it's really a fun topic. Hopefully, with what we talk about tonight, I'll be able to clear up some of the things for you and put you a little more at ease if you're going to be going through this process. Of course, this is general information, so if you are going through the process be sure to speak with your lawyer specifically about any specific quirks of your local USCIS office. And in your case, just things that you might want to expect specifically in your case. But here's some good general information.

When you think of TV, what they typically are showing is the couple goes in all nervous and they ask all these crazy questions and then they answer almost all of them right and then they answer one minor thing not the same way and then they're deported, or something like that. If you've seen the movie Green Card, for an example, it's an old 80's movie or 90's movie, I don't know. That happens in the movie. That's not really what happens in real life. The concept behind the interviews is that they want to see if your marriage is legitimate, if your relationship is real. They are looking to see if you have a fraudulent marriage or not.

For people who have been together a long time, and they know each other well, they would think that, "Hey, we know everything we need to know to be able to pass this interview." It's kind of strange, but we do actually recommend that everyone prepare to some degree because honestly, a lot of married couples just don't always think of these details or they don't have them fresh in their mind. So it's something that you still want to take seriously even if you're a hundred percent clear that your relationship is legit and you know each other very well.

What typically happens is, after the case has been filed, now this is going to be specifically something that's going to happen in an adjustment of status case. In one of our earlier calls, we talked about different ways that the different cases can be filed, so if you're doing an adjustment of status kind of case you'll almost always have this marriage interview. In some other cases where you're filing a marriage petition, and you're going to do the process in a different way, you may have an interview at USCIS, but it's not as common right now. Some people actually do a marriage case and they never actually do this marriage interview, which is kind of an unexpected thing for a lot of people. It's really going to depend on your specific case type.

Let's say you have applied for an adjustment of status and they call you in for an interview. First, they will have already taken fingerprints and run the background check on the immigrant. When they call you in for an interview, both the spouse and the immigrant will need to go to the interview. They send a checklist of the different documents that you should bring. What most of those items are is original documents of the things that you've already submitted photocopies of. For example, a birth certificate, or a passport, all the different types of evidence that show up in your case. You'll want to bring the original ones just in case they ask to look at that. They also ask for even more evidence of your relationship than what you've sent in the beginning. Your lawyer will probably explain to you what types of evidence are good to bring. They just want to keep seeing that it's not just that you got the evidence right before you filed the case and that was it. But, that after a few months with the case being in processing you continue to have evidence of your relationship.

When you're preparing for the interview, it's good to ask about exactly what will happen in the USCIS office. In my local office, here in Indianapolis, and I would say it's kind of the standard operating procedure for different offices around the country, is that you'll go into the interview; they will ask one or both of the people to go back with them to their little office, the particular officer will interview it in their specific office. It really varies a lot by office and by officer, as far as whether they will interview the couple separately or together.

If they're going to interview the couple separately, which is the most common thing we see here in my office, they'll take the immigrant back first, typically. Then they will go over the application that was submitted. So all the different forms, they'll go through and say, "What's your full name? What's your current address? What's your date of birth?" Ask them just to confirm that all the details on the application are correct. They'll also ask details on the forms that have to do with your spouse's information as well. While they're doing that, they'll usually have a big red pen that they're using and they'll check off the different questions. That freaks some people out because they think that they've answered something wrong and they're marking it with the red pen, but it's just so they can keep their place and make sure that they actually confirmed all the different information. Just to make sure they're doing their job the right way. So don't let that throw you off.

When you go in there they will usually, or they should, swear you in to begin with. You'll remain standing and they will have you raise your right hand and swear that you're only going to tell the truth. Most of the offices will also video-tape you. Don't be freaked out by that either; it's not just you specifically. They videotape the interview so that if there's ever any dispute about what was said at the interview, there would be concrete proof of that. I actually think that it's wonderful when they are recording the interviews because that protects you, too. If you had an officer that said you said something you didn't say, well, they've got hard proof of what you really did say. It's actually a good thing, but if you're taken off guard by that, it can be a little unnerving. If you're using an interpreter, they'll swear in the interpreter as well, swearing that they're actually interpreting word-for-word what the person is saying.

After they've reviewed the application with the immigrant they'll start asking questions about the marriage and about the relationship. Every interview is different, every officer is different, with the things that they tend to ask. There are a few really common categories, though, as far as the questions. The most common thing that I see people typically start with are biographical questions. Some of it will stem from the information that was on the application. That's sort of part of the test, hey what's your spouse's date of birth, what's their current address? It should be the same address in almost all cases. If you are living separately for a good reason, then you definitely want to have a lawyer explaining that reason in the application so that they don't get excessively suspicious about that.

They will ask a lot of basic information that a person tends to know about their spouse, like their parents' names, their siblings' names, how many siblings they have, whether they have children, their children's names, when they came to the United States, if they've ever been married before. A lot of just historical things about the other person's life.

They also like to ask questions about the relationship. They'll say, "Hey, when did you first meet? Where was that? What happened? Did you start dating right away? Did you know each other for a while first? Who first asked the other person on a date? Where did you go on your first date? When did you start getting serious and calling each other boyfriend and girlfriend? When did you move in with each other? When did you decide you were going to get married? Did somebody propose to the other person? What was the other proposal like?" And wedding details ... then they like details too, or they like to ask a lot about the wedding itself. Where it took place, who was there, if it was in front of a judge or if it was in a religious ceremony. They'll ask about any kind of party that you would have afterwards. Things of that nature about your relationship. That's definitely another huge category you want to review.

The thing is people, a lot of times, don't necessarily have all that information fresh in their mind, or they have slightly conflicting memories of exactly how everything went down. It's nice to just cover that with your spouse before you go into the interview. We met, it must have been like February, then I guess you asked me out, and about ... Kind of do the calculations together. Not so that you can memorize the facts exactly, just to get on the same page and make sure that you're remembering everything correctly.

Another thing that they like to ask about is your daily routine activities. They tend to ask about who gets up first in the morning, if the other person eats breakfast or not, how long is their commute, where do they work, what are the hours they work or their schedule. If they do anything in the evenings, if there is certain entertainment you watch together, what was the last movie you saw. Details like that about your life.

They might also ask you things about the inside of your house. Where do you have curtains, where are the bathrooms, what color are the walls, how many windows are in your bedroom, something about the appliances in the kitchen or where you plug in your cell phones to charge. Some people are really not that observant and that's pretty normal, so you would want to prepare for that part. You'd want to just walk through your house, or apartment, and just take a good look at everything that's in there. If you're not a very observant person, you might not even notice that there are curtains in the bedroom, or not, or details like that, or wall color. Just kind of make a mental note of everything around you in case you're asked about that.

Then they tend to, during the interview, they'll ask some general questions like that, but during that process they're going to try to drill down on some very specific information that they don't think that you could have studied or planned for. For example, I've seen situations where they ask something like, "Has anyone ever come to visit you since you've been married, when you moved in to this new house that you just mentioned?" The person will answer, "Well, yeah. This person and this person came to visit." They'll get a very specific answer, "Oh, what was that person's name? How long did they stay?" Then they'll go and double check that answer with the other spouse. They'll try to get you to the point where you say something very specific so that they can just spot check that.

So what will happen first is they'll question as much as they want to question that first person until they feel they have good information. Then they'll take that person out into the waiting room and switch and bring the other person back in. Typically, the officer will have the lawyer will stay in the officer's office that whole time so that no one could have any kind of communication between the two different parts of the interview. Then they'll, again, review part of the application just to make sure all the details are correctly entered in the application. Then they ask some more questions to spot check what they already covered with the first person. Usually, the second part is shorter because they're really just trying to double check some of those really specific things that they came up with after doing the first part of the interview. When those things check out, they will be satisfied and end the interview.

There are some offices where it's not very common to do a separate interview like that for the very first interview. In some places they'll actually bring the couple back both together and just ask them general questions at the same time. They'll be similar types of questions, but you'll both be back there together. They might try to talk to only one person to see if that person answers it and it's not as much of a comparing answers sort of thing, just judging the general demeanor of the couple and what they say when they're in there together.

I definitely have noticed that even in offices that do tend to do a lot of separate interviews, when they get behind, they're in a rush, they'll start bringing couples in together just to get things done faster. I wouldn't read anything in to whether you get called back together or separately. Don't let that psych you out at the beginning because it really might have nothing to do with you at all, but just the schedule or how much time, or whether that officer's still in training. You just don't know why they would or why they wouldn't, so don't let that throw you for a loop.

After they've done the questions and they've double checked you, and everything like that, they will, sometimes, tell you right there whether they're going to recommend the case for approval or not. Sometimes they will ask you for more information and say, "Hey, well, you didn't bring this one thing and we still want to see that, or we want to see more evidence of your relationship." Or something like that, and they'll give you a paper that says, "Bring this by this date." Sometimes they'll just say, "Great, well, we need to review this file a little bit more. We'll let you know the decision in the mail." Again, I think a lot of times, everyone of course would love it when they say, "Great, we'll recommend it for approval" right then and there. Because you walk out of there knowing that it's almost certainly going to go through. I should mention that the person who interviews you is not the person who has the ultimate decision about whether the case gets granted or not, but they do have a lot of power. Basically, they recommend a case for approval and then some supervisor has to sign off of it, or something like that. That's why they say, "I'll recommend it for approval instead of, "I'm approving this case." I've actually never had a case that was recommended for approval that wasn't approved. So it's a very good sign.

If they are going to check out some more things or wait for you to respond, it will be super important for you to respond. Because if you don't give them what they wanted within the deadline they gave you, they can just end your case, deny it or consider it abandoned, and then you have to start all over again.

If they say they'll send the decision in the mail, sometimes they do that because there's something suspicious with the case. Sometimes it's just that they haven't gotten a chance to read the whole file yet or to look at your background check and they just need to make sure that everything's okay before they actually issue the decision.

One of the most important things that you need to remember when you're doing the marriage interview is – don't guess! If you can't remember something or you're not sure about something, just say, "I can't remember," or "I'm not sure." People, a lot of times, I'll see in interviews that one spouse will have some elaborate plan for like ... For example, maybe the wife's pregnant and they'll say, "Do you have a baby room planned?" One of the spouses will be like, "Oh yeah, it's going to be like this and we're going to paint it this color." They have all these really specific details and the other spouse, I actually saw this happen in an interview, the other spouse said, "Oh, I don't think we have a plan for that yet." I was actually kind of worried because it was such a different response, but the case got approved on the spot, and I think the officer just thought that kind of proved it was a real marriage even more because one had this idea all worked out and the other one was not on the same page. All couples are like that. So your answers don't have to match exactly, but if there's ever anything you're not sure about just say you're not sure. Where the real problem would be is if you gave a very specific, detailed answer to a question and your spouse gave a very specific, detailed answer to a similar question, but they just totally weren't consistent at all, that's a big problem.

People sometimes want to hide certain details about their case. It might be like, "I've worked without documents before and gotten paid in cash. So instead of saying that, we're just going to say I didn't work at all at this time I was undocumented." Certain things like that they're afraid might come up. It is really important that you just get advice about those issues way before you ever even file the case. You should know whether the factor is going to be a deal breaker for you winning your case or not. Because there are sometimes when people will go in and they're trying to hide something minor, from immigration, and these officers are professional lie detectors. You might look nervous because you're wondering if it's a problem that you did this or that, or maybe you're cutting people's hair from your home for a living and you don't have a license as a hair dresser, or something else that concerns you. By you covering that up, it looks suspicious, they can kind of read you. So get all those questions answered before you even start the case so you don't have any little things that you're trying to hide from the government. They will sense the lie and think you are lying about the relationship, which you're not.

I've seen couples come to see me after they already went to the interview themselves. They did the case themselves, they went to the interview themselves, it went really poorly and then they'll come and see me. For example, there was one couple, and obviously everybody's information is confidential so I'm going to give you a very generalized slightly different version of what happened. One of the spouses had said that one of their relatives lived in the US and the other spouse said that the relative lived abroad, which was ... That's a perfect example of a terrible, terrible situation to have with your interview. How could you make a mistake about that? It was a close relative, and either they live here or they live abroad. There is no way a couple should answer differently about that. So it turns out that the relative actually did live in the United States, but the American spouse said they their relative lived abroad because they just didn't want immigration to poke around in their relative's life. I can understand why someone might be tempted to just kind of hide things like that, but you shouldn't do that at all. Tell the truth. And if you're not sure if the truth is going to disqualify you, then get a lot of help before you start. Because once you have a record like that with immigration, that's pretty bad. By the time people like that come to consult at our firm, they're bringing in a document that says, "We're intending to deny your case because here are all the reasons why we think your relationship is not true. And they make a list of what they specifically find suspicious: "You said this, and your spouse said this, and then you said this…." They have it all written down there and of course there's a videotape to back it up. At that point, there is not much I can do in a lot of cases. We can't go back and say, "Well, the one spouse was lying because of xyz reason." Because they said that under oath, so it's perjury. Plus, why would an officer believe someone who came back and submitted a response that said, "Well, I lied to you before, but I had a pretty good reason to do that. But now I'm telling the truth, which very conveniently benefits me. So approve my case, please." That's why you want to make sure you're on the same page before you go in there.

One thing I definitely think is important to remember is that all officers have very different personalities. Just even in my own office alone, there are people who are kind of always a little bit grouchy, there are people who are very friendly, there are some that kind of joke a little bit, or some of them are more professional, I would say, where they ask the questions, they speak slowly. You never really know what you're going to get, so be prepared for anything and don't worry too much about the demeanor of the officer because it could just be that that is that particular officer's style. It doesn't necessarily mean that it's going to be a problem if the person is very serious with you; just try to be relaxed and confidently answer the questions no matter what. And if you don't remember, say you don't remember. If the officer is casual with you and jokes around, don't get too relaxed, either. Act as you would for a job interview and stay professional. I have seen officers start out joking around, and then turn around and sharply question the couple when their answers got too relaxed and sloppy. Keep that in mind.

Another thing that you definitely want to review ahead of time, I think I didn't quite hit on this before, is to talk about what you did for different major holidays last year, for birthdays, for vacations and family visits. I think a lot of people, and definitely myself included, don't really remember off the top of their head if you ask, "What'd you do last Valentine's day?" I actually just can't remember. Or for my husband's birthday last year, I don't know; I'd have to think about that. If I were on the spot when someone asked me, and I felt a little under pressure, it would be even harder for me to answer that question. Definitely review those major vacations and holidays and parties, and whose family did you visit last year on Christmas, that sort of thing. You definitely want to go over that together when you're starting to review for your interview.

I also recommend you look at the forms that you filled out, just so that you remember exactly what you put down. Of course you're not going to lie, but there are of course times when you remembered that date as, "Okay, I think we moved to that apartment in June of last year." Then if you were asked again a few months later, you might say July because it was pretty close and you can't exactly remember. Well, if you estimated it was June when wrote the application, well then it's June. Don't switch it up, kind of phrase thing the same way, too, just so you don't cast any suspicion unnecessarily on your case because obviously, you've got a legit case. You want to make sure that everything goes through smoothly. However, if you find an actual error in your forms when you are reviewing them, let your lawyer know right away. Depending on the error, it is dealt with in different ways. But what you absolutely don't want to have happen is for the officer to find the error before you disclose it, because it looks like you were trying to hide something.

There are a few things I wanted to talk about as far as people who are at a slightly higher risk of having issues at the interview. One thing I did want to mention, though, is even if you don't have any of these red flags in your situation, please do not think that it's smooth sailing and still do take this really seriously because if you're not able to pass the interview you're not going to be able to win the case. It's very important to make sure everything's in good order to begin with, and like I mentioned before, when people ... Once you start having a bad record with Immigration, the bad evidence against you is going to accumulate, you definitely don't want to let things get out of control before you get help. A lot of times I can't help people once they're in that situation. Sometimes we can clarify and try to clear things up, but you don't want to go there, believe me.

There are some classic red flags that immigration uses to check out certain marriages, put them under more scrutiny, than other marriages. Some of these red flags actually came from a document that was, supposedly, and I think it is true, supposedly it was an internal document from USCIS, actually from back in the day. It actually lists what they call the "fraud indicators." These are things that make them look twice at your case. A lot of these are not very politically correct, I'm just going to say that, but it still doesn't mean that they're not using them as their red flags.

Some of the major things that they might look at would be if you have a large age discrepancy. Say the woman's sixty and the man is thirty-five, or something like that. Even, it doesn't have to be quite that large of an age discrepancy, but they're going to look at that more suspiciously for sure. They are going to look at differences, if you practice a different religion, especially if the religions would be a little bit tougher to be compatible. It's not just that they're two different protestant denominations, but it's something a little bit more with a serious difference. That can be a red flag. If you come from different social classes. Say you have a wealthy immigrant and then you have an American who is really struggling financially, then sometimes they can suspect that maybe the immigrant paid the American to help them out with the case. That can be a little bit of a red flag there. If you have a different level of education, sometimes they look at that. If you have just really different backgrounds somehow. Something about your experience seems like, "How do these people really get along with each other?" and it's kind of a little bit more suspicious to them.

They are going to look, too, at any type of unusual dating history. If you met and then two weeks later, you got married. Or you started dating the week before the person, before their other visa expired or you got married once they got picked up for immigration court. Things that are kind of suspicious timing; they're definitely going to look at more closely. Also, one thing we look at a lot is timelines of your life. Maybe you, and this kind of goes with your suspicious relationship history. Say your spouse broke up with their spouse and then immediately started dating you and then found out they were pregnant with the other person's child and then had the child after you were already together with your partner. That legitimately happens sometimes, but to immigration it's going to look suspicious, very suspicious that your spouse has had a child with someone else while they were together with you. That would be an example of an unusual relationship situation.

Sometimes they look at your divorce, and marriage and divorce timelines. Sometimes people will be divorced right before they're remarried. A lot of times there's a very good reason for that and it's just that there was really no need for them to get divorced, even though they were separated, until they wanted to marry someone else and that's when they got around to doing it. It makes sense, but to immigration that's still something that they could take into consideration that can be a problem.

What happens if you have one of those red flags? I don't want you to think you can't win your case at all, or get too worried, about the fact that you have a potential red flag. It just means that they're going to scrutinize your application more than some other couples. It doesn't mean your application can't be approved. Obviously, there are a ton of happily married couples who have an age discrepancy, or are from different social classes, or practice a different religion. Especially because when Americans are marrying immigrants, yeah, obviously their background is different and that's kind of part of the deal. It's just really important to be aware of those differences so that the cases can be prepared appropriately in a way that overcomes that suspicion.

There's another thing that actually comes again from that fraud indicators document and that I find super interesting. By the way, the document itself is really pretty cool; you can totally Google that if you're interested, or we can find a copy for you. Anyway, the government list says that think it's suspicious if you don't submit enough evidence, but they also think it's suspicious if it's an over-submission. They call it an over-submission, which means you submitted too much relationship evidence. It's kind of funny because it's like, you just can't win with these officers! There is a sweet spot of the right amount of relationship evidence to submit. If you are too paranoid and you're just submitting proof of a bunch of things that you don't really even have to prove, that in itself looks like you're overcompensating for some kind of problem in your case.

So be sure to get advice about your situation, and you

wouldn't want to go way overboard just because you have a particular red flag. Again, that's when you'd want to get legal help from immigration lawyers so that you can submit the right amount of proof and submit convincing proof. There are ways to explain unusual factors and it's just going to be important to explain anything that might be out of the ordinary. Of course they'll be following up with the interview to see if that checks out and sounds reasonable to them.

That's basically what we see with marriage interviews. If the marriage interview does not go well for you, there are a couple different things that could happen. They may just send you, I think we were talking about earlier just about how people can get just a notice of intent to deny. So one option is they can send you a letter saying, "We are planning on denying your case because of this and this reason." And they have to give you specific reasons. They give you a deadline to respond, so they'll say, "If you want to show us proof otherwise, do it within X number of days." Although you do have a chance to respond then, it can be a problem depending on the evidence that they already have.

Another thing that sometimes happens is that you just don't hear anything and the case just seems to lag, and months and months go by and nothing happens, six months go by. The cases I have seen like that have not been cases that we represented a couple from the beginning, but cases where they came to see us later after they've done the case themselves. They typically come after they've noticed that there are people investigating their life in person. We've seen situations where an investigator showed up at like 6:30am at the house of the mother of the American, and just showed her a picture of her supposed son-in-law and said, "Do you know who this is?" Of course the mother was like, "Oh my gosh what's going on?" Or the investigators showed up to see if the couple was getting ready together in the morning at their supposed shared address. They actually do have a team of fraud investigators who sometimes start showing up in particularly suspicious cases. That's very out of the ordinary and it's only going to happen in cases where there are a lot of red flags that would cause you to potentially be investigated by them.

Some people are called in for a second interview, or what they call a fraud interview. If you have to go to a second marriage interview, that is a very, very bad sign and you should not ever go in there without representation and a lot of preparation.

Those are some possible things that might happen, but in the vast majority of cases, if you prepared properly and the case was okay to begin with and you qualify, you'll just have that one interview that you have to get through.

That being said, if you were married for less than two years at the time that the green card is granted, than you'll have to go through another similar process in two years. That first green card will expire in two years and you'll have to do what's called "removal of conditions." The first two-year green card is conditional, it's conditional upon you going through this process of removing the conditions. Basically, what you have to do again is send a different type of application, with more evidence, showing that your relationship is still continuing on and that everything is still legit. If you get through that process, you get a green card that's good for ten years and your status is no longer connected at all to your marriage. You are just a permanent resident like anyone else.

Most people are not re-interviewed at that time, at the two-year mark with the removal of conditions process. If you are ever called for an interview after you've applied for a removal of conditions, that would be another really important time to get a lawyer because if you don't pass the removal of conditions stage, they will try to deport you. It is actually written in the law that USCIS needs to send all of the removal of conditions cases that they deny right on over to Immigration Court where you can try again to defend yourself. A lot of times there are ways to those cases in court.

There are some exceptions, fortunately, some waivers available for people if they are no longer with the American citizen for whatever reason. The spouse may have passed away, or maybe the relationship just didn't work out, which sadly does happen sometimes despite everyone's best intentions for the relationship. There are ways that the immigrant can still get the conditions removed. For most people it's going to be they're just going to, again, show that their relationship was real and that they continue to be together. I just wanted to give you a heads up that you're not totally out of the woods yet once you get your first green card, but definitely it's a wonderful thing when they approve your green card after the interview.

Now that we've talked about those different things, I want to see if anyone had any questions about that? We are also going to be sending our list of classic sample questions that we give to our clients just so they can get a good idea of questions they will see. And so maybe they can practice a few so that they can see if they feel comfortable doing it. You'll see a lot of lists of questions online, and some of them I think are hilarious and I've never ever seen asked. A lot of the lists of questions are drawn from, well sometimes from the person's imagination and they just say crazy stuff that I really don't think they ask people. A lot of times the questions are drawn from fraud interviews that are very, very difficult, after the persons already failed the first interview. If you see something totally bizarre like, what's your favorite position in the bedroom, they're probably not really going to ask you that. Don't freak out too much when you see the questions online because it's just a form of entertainment for people to put this stuff up there and freak other people out.

I do think one reason also that I may not have seen any particularly crazy questions asked is that I think the officers might behave slightly differently when there's a lawyer in the room. I'm not saying ... I think the vast majority of officers would always behave professionally, but you never know, and it sure is nice to have another witness in the room just in case. Fortunately, we don't see a lot of crazy stuff. If you're worried about it, then definitely bring a lawyer with you. With a little bit of preparation, you should be good to go and get through it. Definitely have a celebration after that because it's a wonderful thing when you get to the end of the process, and book your fun trip somewhere abroad now that you can travel freely with your green card!

Megan, is there anyone who, can you explain how they can raise their hands if anyone has a question? I'd be happy to answer questions. Then we'll wrap up this series, this series of classes. Hopefully we'll see you on future calls as well.

Megan: Yeah, definitely. To ask a question just press *6 on your phone now. I will then say the last four digits of your phone number so that you know your line has been un-muted and then you can go ahead and ask your question. Please be sure to introduce yourselves using only your first name, again for privacy, since this call is being recorded. Also, oh I'm sorry we'll just go ahead and go to the first caller right now. I'll give everybody a couple of second to think of their questions. It's just *6.

Okay, it doesn't look like we have any questions this evening, and we completely understand your questions might be private in nature. And plus, I think Clare covered the marriage interview pretty well, so that may have completely satisfied your curiosity. We will send you our list of sample questions soon as well. Please don't hesitate to contact us if we can help you in any way. Our phone number is 317-247-5040.

It's been a pleasure having all of you attend this seminar series with us. Take care everyone, thank you so much for being a part of these calls, and we wish you the best of luck.

Clare: Goodnight everyone.

www.ingramcontent.com/pod-product-compliance
Lightning Source LLC
Chambersburg PA
CBHW060456280326
41933CB00014B/2766